WILLIAM J. BAUSCH

An anthology of
saints

...official, unofficial, and should-be saints

D1600269

TWENTY THIRD 23rd
PUBLICATIONS
NEW LONDON, CT 06320
WWW.23RDPUBLICATIONS.COM

For Dick,
untimely gone

TWENTY-THIRD PUBLICATIONS
A Division of Bayard
One Montauk Avenue, Suite 200
New London, CT 06320
(860) 437-3012 or (800) 321-0411
www.23rdpublications.com

Permissions, Notes, and Credits can be found on pages 224–226.

Library of Congress Cataloging-in-Publication Data
Bausch, William J.
An anthology of saints : official, unofficial, and would-be saints.
p. cm.
Includes bibliographical references.
ISBN 978-1-58595-845-0
1. Christian saints—Biography. 2. Christian biography. I. Title.
BR1710.B38 2012
270.092'2--dc23
[B]
                    2011052979

ISBN 978-1-58595-845-0
Printed in the U.S.A.

CONTENTS

Introduction   1

Prologue

1. The Saintly Chorus   8
2. The Saintly Underground   11
3. The Saintly Contagion   16

Standards

4. St. Jesus of Nazareth   24
5. St. Mary of Nazareth   28
6. St. Joseph of Nazareth   33
7. Sts. Peter and Paul of Rome   36
8. The Desert Fathers of Egypt   40
9. St. Thérèse of Lisieux   46
10. St. Catherine of Genoa and St. Joan of Oregon   49
11. St. Callixtus of Rome and St. John of London   52
12. St. Peter Claver of Spain   55
13. St. Catherine of Siena   59

American Saints

14. Rose Hawthorne   64
15. Barney Casey   67
16. Harriet Tubman   69

17. Thomas Merton   75

18. Dorothy Day   81

19. Pierre Toussaint   88

20. Mychal Judge   90

21. George Washington Carver   94

22. Saintly Snapshots   96

23. Christmas Card Saints   111

New Saints

24. Mother Mary MacKillop   118

25. Matt Talbot   123

26. Miguel Pro   126

27. Blessed Pope John XXIII   129

28. John Newton   135

29. Florence and Edith   138

30. Augustus Tolton   142

31. Victoria Rasomanarivo   147

32. Jean Vanier   149

33. Mother Teresa   153

34. St. Damien of Molokai   157

35. Private Schultz and Sergeant Ponich   161

36. Paul Rusesabagina and the Benebikira Sisters   163

37. Brother André   165

38. Oscar Romero   168

39. Maximilian Kolbe and the Foreman   175

40. St. Dad   179

Legends and Fables

Legends: An Excursus   188

41. The Legend of St. Alexander   191

42. The Legend of Abbot Makarios   196

43. The Legend of St. Dismas   201

44. The Legend of St. Christopher   203

45. The Legends of the Prophet Elijah   206

46. The Legend of St. Jerome   208

47. The Legend of St. Genesius   209

48. A Fable about Thou and I   211

49. A Fable about Papa God   213

50. A Fable about the Hedly Kow   216

51. Mr. Holland and the Holy Shadow   217

A Prayer to End With   223

Notes and Credits   224

INTRODUCTION

Saints are part of our heritage, revered figures of a Christian culture mostly created by popular acclaim until the thirteenth century, when the pope took over. Before television the cult of the saints once dominated the popular imagination. Since television they have been displaced by the rapid, fifteen-minute commercialized celebrities we idolize today. We note the difference between the two. While our present-day secular celebrities point to and celebrate themselves (and the products they sell) the saints point to or wrestle with "Something More" beyond appearances, or frequently "Some *One* More," One who disturbs, beckons, forgives, and loves. They have bought into the "one thing necessary" that Jesus offered to Martha. Saints become mirrors to another reality. That's why Kenneth Woodward is perceptive in saying that saints are those through whom we catch a glimpse of what God is like—and of what we are called to be.

Others have offered their definitions:

> "The saint loves people and uses things. The sinner loves things and uses people." (Sidney Harris)

> "They give more than they receive; they give more than they have." (Bernanos)

"The saints tell us that even in *this* way one can follow Christ." (Rahner)

Finally, the always quotable Oscar Wilde: "The only difference between a saint and a sinner is that every saint has a past and every sinner has a future."

But Woodward remains right: saints point to another dimension of life that we are called to follow.

So traditionally we have our saints, but, in time, familiarity and sentimentality have done them in. Take, for example, the images of our most popular duo, Francis of Assisi and the Little Flower. There he is, plopped in our gardens, wearing a rough cloth garment with a rope for a belt and sandals on his feet, and he's preaching to birds. He's the icon of the devout, the effete, and the crackpots. Thérèse is dressed in her well-laundered Carmelite outfit with a cross on her arm filled with roses, and she is dropping down a rain of rosebuds from heaven. The result of these images is that one gets sort of sweet Disney figures with no hint of the radicalness of their lives, no hint, for example, that Francis, the son of a rich merchant, would stand in the public square, take off all his fine clothes, and walk away naked to embrace Lady Poverty. That's equivalent to a well-heeled kid of today leaving his parents' McMansion, designer clothes, Lexus, and iPad and going off to live with and to serve the poor in Appalachia. And there's no hint that rose-dropping Thérèse suffered from consumption and depression and died at twenty-four, all the while unearthing the graces of the ordinary.

Moreover, in the old days, Catholics were treated to a litany of official saints heavily tilted towards clerics and founders of religious orders, a condition reflecting the fact that the religious orders, already having the inside track, had the time, resources, and money to advance the causes of their heroes. As a result "clerical" spirituality was held up as the ideal, and the saints became those who were celibate, serious, performed miracles, spent their lives in church, and could hardly wait to suffer and die. For the average person that was a hard act to follow, much less imitate. Fortunately, today the interest in making saints has shifted to lay people, and indeed the Vatican has openly asked for such lay candidates.

And the appreciation of the saints has shifted too. Some saints were serious and did have hard lives, but, for the most part, we now realize that they were fairly balanced people, compassionate, funny, and free. Some of our popular saints lived a long time ago. Others lived recently, and still others are among us. We know they're saints because they seem somehow to embody what the gospel is all about. They just don't have the title.

The fact is, saints come from all walks of life and run the gamut of the seven capital sins, being perverse, prideful, lusty, jealous, greedy, and all the rest. Some live holy lives from day one, others are latecomers, some fall easily into grace. Others are dragged there screaming. Some plod ahead relentlessly though steadily to surrender to God, others have an erratic, on-again, off-again love affair. Some are noble from the start, others become noble after years of deceit and shame. But whatever their history, at least once in their lives, they heroically leap beyond their pride, self-absorption, and even the instincts of self-preservation into a fullness of sacrifice, givingness, and love that takes our breath away. Amazing grace envelops them, sometimes like a gentle breeze, other times like a storm. However it happens, we are surprised, edified, and impressed, impressed enough to call them saints whether they are official or not. Some of these saints (official, unofficial, and should-bes) are in this book.

The saints are a colorful lot, and tradition has assigned them particular territories: St. Joseph is helpful if you want to sell your house, Anthony for finding lost objects, Jude for impossible cases, Christopher for travel, Thomas More for legal problems, and so on. Author Lawrence Cunningham also observes:

> In my work on the saints over the years, I have become intrigued by the titles that certain saints in the Byzantine world are given. Thus, Saints Cosmas and Damien are called the "moneyless ones" because they did not charge for their medical services. Saint Marcellus is one of the *akoimetoi*, the "non-resting ones," so named for their assiduous life of constant prayer. I love the title given to those who faced violence without resisting, like the brother Saints Boris and Gleb in Russia—they are the "passion bearers." Perhaps the oddest are the monks at Saint Saba in the ninth century, who were upholders of the veneration of icons. Iconoclastic monks incised lines of scripture on their faces—according to Butler, twelve lines of iambic verse!—so they became known as the *graphtoi*: the "written ones." Two of them were brothers, Theodore and Theophanes.

Some saints who made the calendar were dropped because better scholarship showed that they were misunderstood or without foundation. Think of St. Philomena and St. Christopher. The same Lawrence Cunningham we just quoted tells of the time he received a call from a reporter in Brazil asking if he knew anything about the wildly popular saint, Saint Expeditus. As far as Cunningham could find out, some relics were shipped out of Italy to France with the stencil on the box saying that they were to be "expedited." Somehow the label got attached to the relics, and somehow the cult of "Saint Expeditus" spread to France and Brazil!

This book, as the title indicates, is an anthology. That is to say, it is not an anthology of books about saints but an anthology of my books that, here and there, have directly or indirectly dealt with saints. So while there is much new material here, much has been culled from my previous books and reworked and edited in order to configure to the topic. Thus there will be a mixture of straight biographical reporting and tweaked homilies. Because this is a kind of *vade mecum* or saint-of-the-day type of book, most of the biographies are brief, two or three pages, enough to see who the saints were, why they were, and how they might inspire us. The book is divided into five parts, starting with the Prologue, which contains homiletic material that gives us the larger context of how saints fit into our lives. Then there are the sections devoted to Standard Saints, American Saints, New Saints, and, finally, Legends with a smattering of fables.

This book started out as a series of daily reflections I gave during Lent. I asked the congregation to imagine the sanctuary as a stage (which indeed it is) as each day I presented a saint who came, as it were, out of the wings from one side, stood off center as I told his or her story, and marched off stage to the other side. Since, as I mentioned, the account of each saint is short, the reader may also use this book as a brief daily lenten reflection or simply as a daily or off-again, on-again spiritual reading for any time of the year. Incidentally, the homilist may find here material for preaching.

I end this introduction quoting Graham Greene's words from his powerful novel *The Power and the Glory* on the poor whiskey priest awaiting his execution. The scene is the last morning of his miserable life:

He felt only an immense disappointment because he had to go to God empty-handed, with nothing done at all. It seemed to him, that at the moment, that it would have been quite easy to have been a saint. It would only have needed a little self-restraint and a little courage. He felt like someone who has missed happiness by seconds at an appointed place. He knew now that, at the end, there was only one thing that counted—to be a saint.

PROLOGUE

1

The Saintly Chorus

• A HOMILY •

It is helpful to start off our saint watch with three important reflections. In this first reflection I ask you to think of the feast of All Saints. This feast is clearly a gorgeous paean to God's mercy, to God's all-inclusiveness; and the rousing song "When the Saints Come Marching In" rightly provokes inspiring and truly awesome feelings. Recall the exotic readings proclaimed at this feast, readings that conjure up the great, heavenly panoramic scene of those vast multitudes of 144,000 saints multiplied endlessly. And that endless crowd provokes many marvelous and compelling imageries, none more powerful, I suggest, than that of a heavenly chorus. Yes, close your eyes for a moment and picture yourself standing in that chorus of endless multiples of 144,000 people, singing a song of faith, singing aloud, if you will, the Creed. And then I ask you to be aware of two things that will be operating as each of us belts out our song, and you must read this carefully to catch its meaning.

The first is this: No one believes it all. No one believes it all. Each of us in the chorus is gifted with only a partial understanding of the mystery of God among us; and so, in our large chorus, one sings with great intensity and assurance, another sings with little attention and conviction. Or perhaps today we're caught by the words and melody because we happen emotionally and spiritually to be in a good place. But, another time, in another mental or emotional place, we feel doubtful and alienated, and we can hardly get the words out of our mouths. That's OK. No one believes it all, but, together, we sing more than we can sing alone. Together we sing more than we can sing alone.

And so the saints, you see, the saints are a chorus, a communion that sings what we cannot and believes those parts we cannot accept. They chant the song of faith with us when we can join them, and they hum the song of faith when we cannot. Together, we, the saints of yesterday and today, sing more than we can sing alone, for no one believes it all, but all believe.

The second thing that operates is this: if no one believes it all, so also no one believes all the time. Our journey of faith is seldom smooth and uninterrupted. At times it fluctuates between belief and unbelief. A few years ago a friend of mine lost her son in an automobile accident. She says that she can no longer believe in God, in a God who would let her son lose his life, especially since she and her family are faithful Catholics and good churchgoers. How could God do this to her? There are three responses to this woman.

The first is to say, "Well, if you can no longer believe, you are no longer a Catholic. You no longer belong." That's a harsh view. It denies the seriousness of her loss.

A second response is to say to her, "You haven't really lost your faith. You're just temporarily depressed. Everything will be fine." Everything will not be fine. This is to deny her pain.

But the third response is to honor her losses, the loss of her son, the loss, or at least, the shock to her faith. The fact of the matter is that tragedy has indeed broken her trust in a loving, provident God. Meanwhile? Meanwhile, the community believes for her. The saintly chorus picks up her faltering verses. The collective faith of the saints sustains her though her period of unbelief; and as she slowly encounters these saints of yesterday and today, she will begin to see *their* scars and sense *their* resilience, and they will help her believe once more, in the face of tragic absurdity, in a new and different way. They will help her sing with a different modulation. They will sing the louder the phrases that she can only sing softly, if at all.

So, you see, no one—you nor I—believes it all. And no one here believes all the time. No one accepts every verse, and no one can sing every note all the time. But the chorus does. The chorus, or the community of saints, sings when you and I are unwilling or unable to do so. Peter sang for Doubting Thomas until he could believe again. Thomas sang for Denying Peter until he could embrace again. Monica sang for her son Augustine when he was in his period of sinfulness and unbelief until he could repent again. Clare sang for Francis when he was sad until he was glad again. We are a whole community. We are a chorus of saints. We support each other and we become more than the sum total of our individual selves.

You exhibit the gifts I don't have, and I exhibit those you don't have. You cry the tears I cannot cry and I laugh the laughter you cannot laugh. You believe when I struggle with doubts. I believe when you struggle with doubts. You smile when I am in tragedy. I grieve when you are in joy. Our individual pieces are partial. Our faith, our hope, and our love are quite incomplete. But the feast of the saints, of *all* the saints—past, present, and future, those in heaven, earth, and purgatory—tells us something. This feast gives us support. It reminds us of our faith family, that we belong to a vast community of time and space. It becomes a revelation and a comfort. It tells us a mighty, comforting truth: together we sing more than we sing alone. We are a Communion of Saints.

2

The Saintly Underground

• A HOMILY •

Our second reflection continues the imagery of the Communion of Saints by uncomfortably calling attention to its dark side: that, alas, one whole section of the chorus—by which I mean that the Catholic Church in the West—has collective sore throats and doesn't sing very well anymore. Or, to be explicit, it is in decline. It is well documented that ex-Catholics form the second largest Christian body in the United States. Among them are our family members and relatives, the one out of every ten Catholics who have left. Over the decades the number of nuns has dropped in half. There is a critical shortage of priests. Parishes are closing or merging everywhere. The clerical sex scandal remains an open wound. The bureaucracy of the Church, which protected pedophiles, is stuck in a patriarchal rut where, like our politicians or Wall Street moguls, they protect their turf, talk only to one another, and are out of touch with ordinary people. At least that's how it appears sometimes.

Whatever the reality, this sore-throat segment is unfortunately the church of the headlines, the television, the anti-Catholic screeds, the popular press. But there is, I remind you, a steady hum, a soft persistent underground singing that nevertheless continues. There are low steady voices, grassroots choirs that still sing the songs of faith, hope, and love. This is the underground chorus. This chorus, this Church, is artfully described by Nicholas Kristof in a *New York Times* op-ed article (April 18, 2010). After noting that like the Lehman Brothers' old boys' club, the Vatican old boys' club, as he calls it, is floundering today. Kristof goes on to say:

But there's more to the picture than that. In my travels around the world, I encounter two Catholic Churches. One is the rigid all-male Vatican hierarchy that seems out of touch…Yet there's another Catholic Church as well, one I admire intensely. This is the grass-roots Catholic Church that does far more good in the world than it ever gets credit for. This is the church that supports extraordinary aid organizations like Catholic Relief Services and Caritas, saving lives every day, and that operates superb schools that provide needy children an escalator out of poverty.

This is the church of the nuns and priests [and lay people] in the Congo, toiling in obscurity to feed and educate children. This is the church of the Brazilian priest fighting AIDS…

This is the church of the Maryknoll Sisters in Central America and the Cabrini Sisters in Africa. There's a stereotype of nuns as stodgy Victorian traditionalists. I learned otherwise while hanging on for my life in a passenger seat as an American nun with a lead foot drove her jeep over ruts and through a creek in Swaziland to visit AIDS orphans…

So when you read about the scandals, remember that the Vatican is not the same as the Catholic Church. Ordinary lepers, prostitutes and slum-dwellers may never see a cardinal, but they daily encounter a truly noble Catholic Church in the form of priests, nuns and lay workers toiling to make a difference. It's high time for the Vatican to take inspiration from that sublime—even divine—side of the Catholic Church, from those church workers whose magnificence lies not in their vestments, but their selflessness…

So the point is, the muted singing goes on.

Someone else has noticed this underground chorus. It's a man named Sam Miller, a prominent Cleveland Jewish businessman. He writes:

> Why would newspapers carry on a vendetta on one of the most important institutions that we have today in the United States, namely the Catholic Church?
>
> Do you know the Catholic Church educates 2.6 million students every day at the cost to that Church of 10 billion dollars, and a savings on the other hand to the American taxpayer of 18 billion dollars. The graduates go on to graduate studies at the rate of 92%. The Church has 230 colleges and universities in the U.S. with an enrollment of 700,000 students. The Catholic Church has a non-profit hospital system of 637 hospitals, which account for hospital treatment of one out of every five people—not just Catholics—in the United States today....
>
> Walk with your shoulders high and your head higher. Be a proud member of the most important non-governmental agency in the United States...Be proud to speak up for your faith with pride and reverence and learn what your Church does for all other religions.
>
> Be proud that you're a Catholic.

In other words, remember, amid the din of bad news, that the song goes on and the saints are still marching.

Finally, while we're culling the newspapers, there's another op-ed article in the *New York Times* (September 20, 2010, Ross Douthat) that we need to notice. It wrote of Pope Benedict's visit in 2010 to England to make John Henry Cardinal Newman a saint. Despite the threats of assassination and dangers from the violent anti-Catholic segments, the visit turned out surprisingly well. Despite disagreements and scandals, the pope drew enormous and unexpected crowds. The article said, "They weren't there to voice agreement with Benedict necessarily. They were there to show their respect—for the pontiff, for his office, and for the role it has played in sustaining Catholicism for 2,000 years...." The article continues:

> On Saturday, Benedict addressed Britain's politicians in the very hall where Sir Thomas More, the great Catholic martyr, was condemned to death for opposing the reformation of Henry VIII. It was an extraordinary moment, and a reminder of the resilience of Catholicism, across a gulf of years that's consumed thrones, nations and civilizations. This, above all, is why the crowds cheered for the pope, in Edinburgh and London and Birmingham—because almost five centuries after the Catholic faith was apparently strangled in Britain, their church is still alive.

These positive messages need to be heard. Yes, the Church, as in other eras of history, is hemorrhaging, and the hierarchy is in need of reform. But that is not the only church we know—or are. We don't dine with popes, cardinals, and bishops. We do not live in the Vatican. We ordinary people live in a church of St. Vincent de Paul societies; soup kitchens; Catholic Workers in Harlem; Mother Teresa's nuns in Asbury Park; Martin House in Trenton; Food for the Poor; Catholic Relief Services; jail, hospital, and shut-in visitors, a church where ordinary people like ourselves gather for worship and quietly carry out works of compassion and mercy in our own neighborhoods where secret heroisms thrive. Our theme song is the classic and effective: "Gather the folks, tell the story, break the bread, share the love." Who does that better than the local chorus, the local church?

Let me share an instance of a subversive song. Nobel Prize-winning author Alexandr Solzhenitsyn was imprisoned for a number of years in Soviet labor camps. One day, at the point of despair, he dropped his shovel, sat down on a bench, and closed his eyes. He did not care anymore if a guard killed him. Hearing footsteps, he looked up to see an elderly prisoner, who knelt down and with a stick scratched the sign of the cross into the dirt. In that moment Solzhenitsyn realized that he was not alone. The sign of the cross scratched in the dirt by another prisoner gave him the hope to go on. For the moment, the two were church, for, as Jesus said, "Where two or three are gathered together in my name, there I am in the midst of them."

Yes, in a time of bad press, we need to be aware that the Jesus of the shepherds, fishermen, outcasts, farmers, peasants, prisoners, and ordinary people lives among us. We still hear his voice, feed at his table, and do his deeds all over the world. We need that public three-percent face of the church, the pope, and the bishops, who anchor us to the ancient traditions and keep the chorus together, but they also need us, the vast unsung church, the one that, as always in history, when people are in distress and despair, is there to quietly scratch crosses in the dirt.

As saints, we need to continue to sing, however softly. It's our calling.

3

The Saintly Contagion

• A HOMILY •

Our final reflection in this prologue is this: the one thing we know about holiness is that it is catching. In these pages we will meet the worldly Thomas Merton and his first impacting encounter with a pious Catholic family. We'll meet Pope John XXIII, who credits his parents with showing him how to live a holy life. There is convert Edith Stein, who reported that she converted, under the impulse of grace, after reading Teresa of Avila's autobiography. Teresa herself remarks in the same book that reading Augustine's *Confessions* was a turning point in *her* life. Augustine marks his conversion happening after reading a codex of Paul's letters. What a chain: Paul to Augustine to Teresa to Edith.

But more to our own times here is modern author and convert Robert Ellsberg who testifies to this truth. He writes:

> I was searching for something more. It was that search that led me, many years ago, to drop out of college and make my way to the Catholic Worker, a "house of hospitality" on the Lower East Side of Manhattan.
>
> At the age of nineteen, I was eager to experience something of life firsthand, not just from books. I was tired of living for myself alone and longed to give myself to something larger and more meaningful. I had a pretty good idea of what I was *against*; I wanted to find out what my life was *for*.
>
> I remained at the Catholic Worker for five years. By the time I left I had found much of what I had been

seeking, and perhaps more. Among other things I had become a Catholic. The attraction of Catholicism had little to do with doctrine or the church's teaching authority, of which I comprehended very little. It had much more to do with the wisdom and example of its saints.

So this calls for some quick sketches of everyday contagious saints who prove the point.

Jack Casey is a volunteer fireman and ambulance attendant who, as a child, had to have some of his teeth extracted under general anesthesia. Jack was terrified, but a nurse standing nearby said to him, "Don't worry. I'll be right here beside you no matter what happens." When he woke up from the surgery, she had kept her word and was still standing beside him. Nearly twenty years later his ambulance crew was called to the scene of an accident. The driver was pinned upside down in his pickup truck, and Jack crawled inside to try to get him out of the wreckage. Gasoline was dripping onto both Jack and the driver, and there was a serious danger of fire because power tools were being used to free the driver. The whole time the driver was crying out about how scared he was of dying and Jack kept saying to him, recalling what the nurse had said to him so many years before, "Look, don't worry. I'm right here with you. I'm not going anywhere."

Later, after the truck driver had been safely rescued he was incredulous. "You were an idiot!" he said to Jack. "You know that the thing could have exploded and we'd both have been burned up." In reply Jack simply said he felt he couldn't leave him. That's the way sainthood works. A nurse saying "I'll be right there beside you" becomes the action of a man who stays beside a stranger. Saints beget saints.

Next, go back to June 27, 1880, in Tuscumbia, Alabama. There a delightful, darling little girl was born, healthy and well. But she soon picked up some kind of fever of undisclosed origin, and before she was a year and a half, she could not hear and she could not see. She was now both deaf and blind.

This girl, of course, was Helen Keller. Her family, as you know, if you've read her story or have seen the play or movie *The Miracle Worker*, overcompensated for her handicap by spoiling her so rotten that she became an uncontrolled, uncontrollable hellion of a child. Later on she tried to describe this period of her life, what it was like to be imprisoned in her body, not hearing or seeing. At one point she likened her condition to a ship that was in a dense fog with no compass, no plumb line, no nothing. She waited like that ship in the fog, she said, fighting back anger and rage, being overcome by the enormity of the obstacles she knew she faced. She waited and waited until March 3, 1887, the day when the fog began to lift. On that day she wrote:

> The most important day I remember in all my life is the one in which my teacher, Anne Mansfield Sullivan, came to me. I am filled with wonder when I consider the immeasurable contrast between the two lives which it connects.
>
> On the afternoon of that eventful day I stood on the porch, dumb and expectant. I guessed vaguely from my mother's signs and from the hurrying to and fro that something unusual was about to happen. So I went to the door and I waited on the steps. The afternoon sun penetrated the mass of honeysuckle that covered the porch and fell on my upturned face. My fingers lingered almost unconsciously on the familiar leaves and blossoms which had just come forth. I

did not know what the future held, of marvel or surprise for me. Anger and bitterness had preyed upon me continually, and left me with a great struggle. I felt approaching footsteps. I stretched out my hand as I supposed it to be my mother. But someone took it, and I was caught up and held close in the arms of someone who had come to reveal all things to me. And, more than all else, to love me.

If you remember the play or movie, this Annie Sullivan did give the child enormous love and firm discipline. This was a little wild animal of a child, and Annie's combination of very tender and warm love and a very stern and uncompromising discipline touched this girl deeply and made her into a human being and a very great one at that. Even such—at times—a bitter and cynical soul as Mark Twain, who got to know Helen Keller, reckoned her and Napoleon as the two most interesting figures in the nineteenth century, Napoleon because he had conquered the world in his quest for power, and Helen Keller because she had conquered her own physical limitations to become a beautiful and noble lady.

There's Leon. Leon was a young man, a lad, really, growing up in Poland during the Second World War. Leon and his family were Jews. He had seen his parents and his other relatives and friends killed or hauled off to the concentration camps by the Nazis. Little Leon fled to a nearby farm and hid there. Still he was only a boy and could not fend for himself. And so one day he introduced himself to the farmer. The farmer and his wife happened to be very sensitive people, very good Catholics, and they hid Leon for years. They fed him, clothed him, and took care of him even though, had they been caught doing so, they would have been executed immediately.

After the war, once grown up, Leon moved to the United States. He went to school, was a brilliant student, and became a rabbi. To this day, Leon, as an older man now, tells of his childhood and the people who saved him, and he shares with his Jewish friends his great appreciation and empathy for the Catholic Church because those Catholics of long ago had been so good to him.

In another camp was a Dr. Boris Kornfeld, a medical doctor in a Siberian prison camp. He was Jewish, but he began to notice one of the prisoners, a Christian, a man of quiet faith. The man seemed to find great strength in that horrible place by reciting the Lord's Prayer over and over. We don't know that man's name. We only know that his witness and his friendship began to change Dr. Kornfeld. One day, they brought a guard to Kornfeld for treatment. The guard's artery had been cut in a knifing, and he was bleeding to death. Dr. Kornfeld knew that he could save the man, but he thought about letting him bleed to death. He considered suturing the artery in such a way that it would fail later. Then he caught himself horrified by his own thoughts. He remembered his friend who prayed, "Forgive us our sins as we forgive those who sin against us."

Dr. Kornfeld began to hold himself and others to a higher standard. He turned in an inmate who had stolen food and who had thereby endangered the lives of other prisoners. As a result, he found his own life in danger. He spent more and more time at work, where he felt a little safer. One day they brought a prisoner to him, a man who had cancer. The man was seriously ill, but his greatest suffering was spiritual. Kornfeld looked into his eyes, and saw only emptiness and misery. And so Dr. Kornfeld began to tell the man about his Christian friend who had prayed the Lord's Prayer, and he began to tell him about his own awakening faith. They became friends.

That night, a prisoner sneaked into Kornfeld's room and took his revenge. He bashed Kornfeld's head with a rock, and Kornfeld died. That should have been the end of the story, but it was not.

The cancer patient remembered what his newfound friend, Dr. Kornfeld, had said. He recovered from his illness, and began his own journey of faith. He became a Christian. He survived that prison camp, and he began to write about his experiences there. His name was Aleksandr Solzhenitsyn, whom we mentioned in the last chapter. Solzhenitsyn's writings turned a spotlight on Soviet cruelty, and they played some small part in the fall of the Evil Empire.

The point of all these stories is summed up in the one about a childless couple who had raised their orphaned nephew, David, who was now leaving them for college. They were at the railroad station. David looked at his aunt and uncle. She, with hands chapped and hard from selling fruit and vegetables outdoors in all kinds of weather, face ruddy and round and invariably smiling, the heavy body more accustomed to a half-dozen sweaters at one time than a single coat, her hair the color of moonlight now, but the dark eyes still bright.

He, with his slight, wiry body strong and bent from lifting too many fruit and vegetable crates for too many years, the wind-burned skin, the swarthy face, the wry mouth; the childless couple who had taken the orphan David into their home, rearing him since the age of seven yet refusing to be called Mamma and Papa for fear he would forget his real parents.

David grabbed their rough peddlers' hands in his smooth student ones. "How can I ever repay you two for what you've done for me?" His uncle spoke gently, "David, there's a saying, 'The love of parents goes to their children, but the love of these children goes to their children.'" "That's not so," protested David, "I'll always be trying to…". His aunt interrupted, "David," she said, "what your uncle means is that a parent's love isn't to be paid back. It can only be passed on."

Like holiness.

STANDARDS

4

St. Jesus of Nazareth

Startled at the title of this chapter? We're not used to thinking of Jesus as a "saint." *Saint* Jesus sounds so odd. After all, he is the source of holiness not the product. Yet the word "saint" is a translation of the word for holy, and it's time to think of Jesus in terms of holy, a holy man. I say it's time because we have spent too many centuries defining and worshiping Jesus, literally killing one another over right doctrine (ortho-doxy) about him. We have spent too many centuries on the question of salvation (our liturgical prayers are heavily weighted with asking Jesus to "count us among those you have chosen") and not enough on the question of witnessing to him for its own sake. Simply put, the issues of dogma, worship, and salvation have too often overwhelmed fidelity, discipleship, and sacrifice. Not that the former are not critical issues—they are—but they are far from the whole story. The fuller story is following Jesus; yet, among theologians and especially preachers, this often comes second to orthodoxy and loyalty to the Church. One will be called on the carpet for denying the Trinity but not for gross and hurtful unkindness. "The Church teaches" replaces, "If you were a follower of Jesus, this is what you would do, how you would live." The fact is that the Church often gets in the way of Jesus, and the stories of lives of the saints are a corrective to that. The saints bring us back to essentials. One, for example, thinks of St. Francis of Assisi, living in a time of terrible political and ecclesiastical corruption, who cut to the gospel chase.

So if following St. Jesus, the Holy Man, is what Christianity is all about, let us look to some basics of his teachings and examples that identify his true disciples. We find these teachings and examples in the gospels. The writers of these gospels, writing in hindsight, tried to capture what Jesus' first followers knew and felt about him, what they learned from him. The evangelists, living in a storytelling culture, no matter how they embellished the Jesus stories they heard or how they invented others, did so in order to distill in a memorable way what those eyewitnesses told them. And, to oversimplify, let us list five things they found out about the Holy Man.

Jesus was single-minded. "I come to do the will of my Father who sent me." "Not my will but thine be done." This total single-mindedness led him at times to be testy. He snapped at his disciples for being so dull headed, called the Pharisees "blind guides," the Phoenicians "dogs," and his debaters "liars." And those who like to contrast the harsh God of the Old Testament with the gentle God of the New have never really paid attention to the unnerving stories Jesus told where the Son of Man casts evildoers into eternal fire (Mt 13:42); the Lord [God] hands over the unjust servant to the torturers (Mt 22:13) and tosses the man without the wedding garment into the outer darkness (Mt 22:213), and does the same to the parsimonious servant (Mt 25:30); cuts into pieces the faithless servant (Mt 24:51); has his enemies slaughtered in his presence (Lk 19:27); casts into eternal darkness those who did not do the corporal works of mercy (Mt 25:46); destroys nasty tenants (Mk 12:9), and declares that unbelievers will have to endure God's wrath (Jn 3:36). Some sweet Jesus! Well, the truth is that holy people, precisely because they are holy and single-minded, lose their cool at times and we'll find this same tendency in the lives of the saints.

Jesus was inclusive. While other rabbis had table-fellowship meals, they were with those of their own kind. For Jesus, the table was open to everybody, so much so that his enemies accused him of eating with publicans and sinners. Jesus shocked everyone by touching the untouchable leper, thereby taking on his ritual uncleanness. Crossing lines, he spoke to the woman at the well and cured the hated Roman centurion's servant. He told a story about a Samaritan who was good. Jesus the holy man lived, taught, and practiced inclusiveness. His life said that all were children of the heavenly Father.

Yet some of those who call themselves his followers exclude others, and often violently. History is full of such betrayals of Jesus. Think of those Christians who killed one another in religious wars, those who justified and defended the Jim Crow laws in the South, the fundamentalist Christians carrying signs saying that God hates homosexuals. The divisions continue. On the other hand in these pages we will meet saints who were faithful to the Teacher: Abba Abraham, who left the desert to reclaim a prostitute; Hotel keeper Paul Rusesabagina, who saved many in the awful genocide in Rwanda; Rose Hawthorne, who ministered to cancer patients of every color and belief; Pope John XXIII, who touched the hearts of some atheistic communists; Dorothy Day, whose Catholic Worker movement shelters, clothes, and feeds all who come to it; Thomas Merton, who reached across the divide to the East. You can be a believer if you are exclusive, but you can't be a follower.

Jesus practiced forgiveness and taught it as a cornerstone of his ministry, saying that it should happen seventy times seven times. He forgave the woman caught in adultery, Zacchaeus the tax collector, Peter the denier, the people who were killing him. He left us the parable of the Prodigal Son. Yet, some who would never deny any article of the Creed seek revenge and exact extreme punishment. One thinks of Oscar Wilde's remark, "As one reads the pages of history, one is appalled, not at the crimes of the wicked but at the punishments of the just."

Jesus did good deeds and showed compassion—think of his kindness to children and the sick, his feeding of the hungry crowds. Think of his story about Dives who had Lazarus at his door, Jesus' teaching about giving one's coat to one who asks only for one's tunic, going the extra mile, his praise of the widow's mite. He made these things the criteria for those worthy of heaven. No matter what the controversies over faith versus good works, Jesus was clear that if one did not feed the hungry, give drink to the thirsty, clothe the naked, and visit the imprisoned, that person was not fit to be with those who did. Think then of those who live only for themselves. Think of the excessive greed that has caused our recession. Then think of Damien of Molokai and Mother Teresa. They shared the same label, the same worship, the same creed as some of those who are greedy, and they too believed in the Holy One, but they are saints, holy ones, because they *followed* the Holy One.

Finally, *Jesus was willing to sacrifice himself to be true to his beliefs*. His eating with sinners cost him acceptance. His preaching cost him the ire of his enemies. His clinging to his Father's will cost him his life. His teaching was: "He who would save his life will lose it. Whoever loses his life for the sake of the kingdom will find it." He practiced that. So, in his name, did the saints. Think of Stephen, Sebastian, Agnes, Polycarp, Thomas More, Thomas Becket, Oscar Romero, Paul Miki and his companions (twenty-six sixteenth-century crucified Japanese martyrs), Dietrich Bonhoffer, Franz Jagerstatter (devout husband and father who refused to take the oath of loyalty to Hitler), Miguel Pro, and countless others.

The holy man, Jesus, inspired all this. It was the life he lived setting a pattern of single-minded fidelity to his Father. His love was broad, building bridges instead of walls. He was compassionate and identified with the marginalized. He reached out to them and told his followers to do the same. His compassion included a healing and redemptive forgiveness. He lived his convictions and died for them. That's how it must have appeared to some first-century, rough fishermen or to a bleeding woman reaching out to touch his hem. Here was someone who was his own man, a man of deep piety who walked the walk and talked the talk. So, for the moment, forget all the orthodox grand titles: Lord of Lords, God from God, Messiah, Savior, Redeemer, King. Forget for the moment all the stylized or saccharine pictures of a cosmic Christ or a sweet Jesus. Think simply of Saint Jesus and cry out, "St. Jesus of Nazareth, who prayed for Peter (Lk 22:32) and is always interceding with the Father, pray for us."

5

St. Mary of Nazareth

Jesus had a mother but we really know so little about her. We don't know where or when she was born or where and when she died, but we can place her in history. We do know where she lived and who were some of her friends and family. With that meager information, the question we have to explore is why does she, above all the saints, persist through the ages? What is her appeal? For an answer we must consciously put aside all the trappings, affections, and titles the centuries have heaped upon her and go back to the bare bone hints we get of her in Scripture. Sticking solely to the New Testament we catch some profound insights of a woman on the same human journey we travel and there we discover the secret: Mary survives because she is us.

When we first meet her, Mary is the object of an ugly rumor: she is pregnant without a husband. Her fiancé, Joseph, is of a mind, officially, to deny her and anything about the pregnancy and put her at a distance. That she was innocent, invaded by the Spirit, was not believed. So right away, people down the ages who have suffered from false rumors, who have had their reputations soiled, who have been misunderstood and maligned, or who are unwed mothers, have identified with her.

Then, too, there was her very human anxiety and fear. What's this all about anyway—this mother of God business? "How can this be?" she asked the angel incredulously, "What does God want? What about Joseph? How can this happen? How can I do this?" Confused and scared and full of questions, Mary is all those people throughout the ages who have cried out, "How can I tackle this challenge? How can I survive? What does God want of me?"

When her son was born, shepherds and angels rejoiced, but powerbrokers seethed and conspired to kill her baby. They wanted his life, his spirit. And parents today and down the ages, faced with so many soul assassins, have identified with Mary. They know well enough that there are people out there waiting to kill their children. The people who are waiting to sell their children drugs, the media that glamorizes uncommitted sex, the hawkers with cash registers for hearts who teach them that we *do* live by bread alone, the soul snatchers of false values—all are after their children to kill their spirits. Parents know what Mary knew and fear what she feared.

Mary has to flee with her husband and child and become a refugee in a foreign land and immediately joins the countless displaced persons, the homeless huddling in the world's doorways and sleeping on the nation's grates, and the millions of millions of refugees walking the earth today—these lowly who need to be lifted up. They are cousins under the skin, and they can identify with Mary.

Mary loses her child when he is an adolescent. She becomes every parent, every teacher, every mentor in history who can't communicate with a teenager, who loses them to gangs or drugs, whose kids have joined the small army of runaways roaming the streets, exploited by the sex trade, abused and beaten. Many can identify with Mary here.

At some point—we don't know when—this wife and mother became a widow. She buried her husband, and everyone who has lost a spouse, cried Mary's tears, felt the gnawing void in their belly, and returned to an empty bed can identify with her.

When her son is old enough he leaves home to begin his mission, and he leaves a widowed mother behind. Suddenly every mother and father who see their children grow up and leave them behind—especially those in nursing homes—know what she is feeling in her heart.

When she walks the streets now that she is alone, she has to give way to the rough Roman soldiers and leering men passing by. She has to move quickly and live in the shadows. As a minority woman in an occupied territory, as a widow with no man around, she is always subject to sexual and physical exploitation and discrimination. Everyone with no rights, every minority figure who has to swallow their pride, everyone ever called "nigger" or "spic" or "wop" or "fag" can identify with Mary.

When she hears rumors that her son is preaching nearby, she goes with some relatives to see him but can't get near because of the crowds. She has to be content with sending word that she's out there on the fringe. When Jesus is told that his mother and relatives want to see him, he, gesturing to the crowd, asks, "Who are my mother and brothers and sisters? Everyone who does the will of God is my mother and brother and sister."

It sounded like a put down, a message to tell his mother to go home, but she read it for what it said, what she always knew: her glory was not primarily that she was his biological mother, but that she was closer to him than anyone else because she loved God and did his will, even when she didn't understand it. And every little person on the sideline, off-center, on the fringe who doesn't understand what's going on, but simply clings fast to God's will, can identify with Mary.

And then that son is caught—betrayed by one she had had over for dinner many a time—brought to a mock trial, beaten and humiliated and hung on a public cross. She arrives in time to see him hanging there, every inch of her mind and body straining to go to him, but she is forced by the soldiers to keep her distance. And suddenly, every parent who has seen their child on a cross, every parent who has seen their child carted off to prison, every parent who wants more than anything else in the world to help their grown children who are dealing with alcoholism, living in sin, raising their children with no religion and not even having them baptized, going through a divorce—every parent who witnesses such "crucifixions" but who must keep their distance, who are *told* to keep their distance, can identify with Mary and have to pray and suffer in silence.

And finally she cradles the broken dead body of her only son in her arms and sobs uncontrollably and there she is once more: every parent who has lost a child, any friend who has lost a friend, any classmate who has lost a classmate through overdose or gunshot can identify with Mary of the Pietà.

This is the woman—this pilgrim who savored the ups and downs of life—*this* is the ageless woman who has been given to us as a legacy. "Son, behold thy mother." And here we are in our age beholding her. But it's good to remember that we're beholding her *now*, now that it's all over. We tend to imagine Mary as she has been romanticized. We see her clothed with the sun, the moon beneath her feet, stars around her head, dressed in medieval robes, winged cherubs to do her bidding, against a background of Italian villas. We can almost hear her being whisked up into heaven to the sound of Handel's *Messiah*.

But we should understand that all this is metaphor, figures of speech, storytelling. What it all means to say—all this heavenly glamour—is that Mary who is Everywoman, Everyman, is blessed now because, unblessed in many ways in life, she remained faithful. In all of the unfairness of life, she clung to God. In virginity, in motherhood, in widowhood, at home, a wanderer in a foreign land, with live child, with dead child, she clung to God.

So she becomes a woman for all ages and identifies with all people, and that is the secret of her enduring popularity and her appeal. And the later Church elevates her, not because she started out as great and traveled a privileged path, but because she was a handmaid of the Lord and traveled the lowly path. But then, he who is mighty has done great things for her. He has lifted her up when she was down, fed her when she was hungry, and because she responded to his loving invitation wherever life would lead her, saw to it that all generations would call her blessed.

That's what we continue to do: calling this woman of our flesh and blood, our experience, blessed. Which is not honoring someone far away and high above us. No, we're calling blessed someone near and right with us at every human step. And she is hope. She is promise fulfilled, humanity completed, faithfulness rewarded. Simply put, she is us at the end of the journey we are traveling. That is why Mary is so compelling. She is indeed a Woman for All Times and All Seasons.

6

St. Joseph of Nazareth

"This is how the birth of Jesus Christ came about." With these words, St. Matthew begins to introduce the world to Saint Joseph. His name is quickly mentioned four times in a few verses in Matthew's gospel and yet, the truth is, we know so little about him. Nevertheless, even from the meager hints we have about him, it would appear that three things initially stand out about this man from Nazareth: he was perplexed, he was marginal, he was a loser.

He was perplexed. His fiancée was pregnant by another man as far as he could tell. He was torn between his trust in her and what seemed like the obvious facts. He was afraid to take her as his wife, a fear the angel duly noted. Between his knowledge of Mary's condition and that dream of his, he spent tortured days and sleepless nights. There was so much he didn't understand.

He was marginal. He comes and goes so quickly in the gospel stories. Gone and forgotten. There is not even one recorded word of his. Everyone else has something to say: the angel, Mary, the shepherds, Herod, the Magi. But not Joseph. Silence. The spotlight, literally and figuratively, shines on Jesus and Mary. He's not even the child's real father. He's a stepdad. The manger scene often puts him in the shadows. Like the old Lone Ranger series, everyone asks, who was that masked man? We really don't know.

Finally, he was, to put it mildly, a loser. He had to fall in love with a mystic, someone claimed by a higher power. He had to struggle with doubts and desperately search for answers. He lost his wife to God, as it were. Then he, the so-called great family man, lost his only son and had to go looking for him down the alleys and byways of Jerusalem. Finally, he lost his life somewhere between that search for Jesus and Jesus' start of his public ministry. He was gone. Deceased. He left his wife a widow and his son fatherless. Not a great track record. Joseph the loser.

And yet in our times, laced with fears of depression, terrorism, a seemingly endless war, recession, it is this Joseph who, of all the characters who appear in the Nativity story, speaks to many, resonates with many, identifies with many—with us.

Let us look: we said that Joseph was perplexed, and we also are perplexed. There is so much we don't understand about today's world: the ramifications of human cloning, why other peoples hate us, why 9/11 happened, why families break up, why children kill children, why parents divorce, why a child is on drugs. Why, in short, is there so much evil? We are perplexed. But notice, Joseph, the also perplexed, just didn't stand there paralyzed. His perplexity did not stop him from doing what he could. He led his pregnant wife on a long caravan journey to Bethlehem, found a place for her to have a baby, fled with his family to Egypt like the Trapp family fleeing the Nazis, supported them by his handiwork, taught his son a trade. The point is, in spite of so much he didn't understand, he did what he could to make this world a better place. He did his duty. Simply, faithfully, loyally, dependably. To that extent, Joseph speaks to all who are perplexed, and he says, "Do what you can do to be caring, compassionate, and helpful. Stay loyal and faithful to your beliefs and convictions. Do your duty. *You* make this world a better place."

We said he was marginal, but remember: this man also had dreams that sustained him—just like another marginal person of the twentieth century who proclaimed, "I have a dream." As such Joseph speaks to today's hopeless, today's marginal people. Not just those shunted aside because of the color of their skin or their nationality, but the slow, the unpopular, the unattractive, the disappointed, the poor, the hurting, those considered on the fringes of nerdville, beyond the social pale—anyone who desperately dreams that things could be better. Joseph speaks to them all. He reminds them to hold on to and cherish their dreams. Have faith, he would say. Look, as it turned out, Mary of Nazareth became queen of heaven, Jesus, the infant in danger of death, became Savior. And Joseph himself, dreamer that he was, eventually emerged from the shadows so that the whole world now knows him as Saint Joseph. So have faith in God. Remember Joseph. Cherish your dreams.

Finally, we said he was a loser, a man who knew loss. He speaks deeply to all others who are losers, who also have suffered loss, and, since he appears especially visible at Christmas time, we should invoke his memory then. He knows, for example, that Christmas will be hard on the thousands upon thousands who have lost their jobs in the ripple effects of a prolonged recession, who will experience a leaner holiday, smaller meals, fewer presents—perhaps feelings of failure and desperation. He knows that there will always be Christmases that will be sad for those who have lost family members and friends in the World Trade Center attack, the Afghanistan or Iraqi wars, or other disasters. With sorrow he sees that there will be empty places at the festive table, empty spaces under the tree, empty beds, empty hearts, perhaps a photograph with a vigil candle on the coffee table. It is so unbearably sad. Joseph, who almost lost a wife and did at one time lose a son, knows the feeling. But, again, he also knew that God would have the last word, that God in time could make loss flower into compassion, service, and growth. That, although scars would remain and grief would now and then openly assert itself, loss would be the seeding place of quiet greatness.

So during Advent Matthew, who gives us the birth story from Joseph's perspective, presents us with a role model, a man for our seasons. He asks in effect, are you like Joseph, perplexed, marginalized, hurting over losses? Let Joseph's steadfastness and example be yours for he is the kind who many times would have the occasion to utter this ancient Gallic prayer.

As the rain hides the stars,
as the autumn mist hides the hills,
as the clouds veil the blue of the sky—
so the dark happenings of my life hide
the shinning of Thy face from me.
Yet if I may hold Thy hand in the darkness,
it is enough.
Even though I may stumble in my going,
Thou dost not fall. Thou dost not fall.

7

Sts. Peter and Paul of Rome

Firmum est cor meum—"my heart is firm or faithful"—are the words on the seal of the North American College, the American seminary in Rome. It's a fitting motto for us to remember as we recall our founding fathers Peter and Paul, because, if they were not born in Rome, they died there.

Yes, Peter and Paul—one called by the Sea of Galilee and the other on the road to Damascus; one the blue-collar fisherman and the other a learned scholar—are founding apostles, and we celebrate them as any country or corporation or organization celebrates the people whose genius gave the original vision and supplied the witness and hard work to make a lasting contribution. We link them together because the two of them single-handedly cemented the foundation of the Church and literally bet their lives on its future.

Some facts. We know for sure that these two did not establish the church in Rome—it was already there when they arrived, founded by one of the other apostles or disciples of Jesus—but we also know for sure that Peter and Paul went there to take their message to the center of civilization, and they died there as the Church's two preeminent apostles—thus enhancing Rome's preeminence—one crucified upside down and the other beheaded. They gave their lives, these two, for the One who gave his life for them. St. Paul was buried beneath the church we know today as St. Paul's outside the walls and St. Peter is buried, of course, under St. Peter's. We know this because for centuries architects have always wondered why they built the first church on such an uncongenial spot of land that required tons of fill dirt to make the ground even when there was already level ground not too far away. Except, of course, that that particular spot, from the very beginning, must have been special.

Investigations in the past century have uncovered the cemetery of Emperor Diocletian and a Christian section and a box of bones which—according to the graffiti on the walls, turned out to be Peter's—buried directly, with mathematical accuracy, layers and layers down, beneath the high altar of St. Peter's. So now we know why they built the church in such an awkward place. It was ground hallowed by the presence of Peter's grave. We know all these things. What we don't know is when all this happened, when Peter and Paul gave their lives for Jesus. Certainly it was not on the same day.

So, as usual the early Christians were inventive. They solved that mystery by taking advantage of what was already there, namely a secular feast day. They chose June 29 for Peter and Paul's deaths because June 29 was already being celebrated as the day

Rome was founded by Romulus. The message was that if Romulus founded an old empire, Peter and Paul laid the foundation for a new one: the Christian Church, which, like the Roman Empire, quickly spread all over the world.

We know other things too about Peter and Paul. They were flawed men who had their names changed: highly significant in those days. One was weak ("Depart from me for I am a sinful man, O Lord") and the other a hothead ("I persecuted the church of Christ"). But Simon was summoned to go beyond his historical weaknesses and become Peter, a rock on which the church would rest. Saul was summoned to go beyond his fervor as a persecutor squelching the new movement and become Paul, apostle to the Gentiles, a promoter of the new movement.

Unlikely candidates for founding fathers, but maybe G.K. Chesterton had it right when he wrote: "All the empires and the kingdoms have failed because of this inherent and continual weakness, that they were founded by strong men and upon strong men. But this one thing, the historical Christian Church, was founded on a weak man and for that reason it is indestructible. For no chain is stronger than its weakest link." So we remember them. We remember them for the same reason anyone has founder days: we look back and we ask, "Can we recapture their original genius and insights? Can we recapture once more the vision that urged them on and made them tick? We seemed to have strayed."

One example will do. The full title of Prince Charles, the future king of Great Britain, is "His Royal Highness Prince Charles Philip Arthur George, Prince of Wales and Earl of Chester, KG, KT, GCB, OM, AK, QSO, PC, ADC, Duke of Cornwall and Duke of Rothesay, Earl of Carrick, Baron of Renfrew, Lord of the Isles and Prince and Great Steward of Scotland." When Jesus was crucified, *his* title, scratched on a simple wooden piece attached to the cross, was: "Jesus of Nazareth, the King of the Jews." And when Peter and

Paul were martyred in Rome, their titles were simply "apostles." The grander titles would come later: Holiness, Supreme Pontiff, Eminence, Most Reverend, Your Grace, My Lord, Monsignor, and the rest.

You catch the difference in this comparison. Before the titles, Peter was walking along the street when, as you may recall from the book of Acts (3:6), a lame man begged alms, and Peter famously replied, "Silver and gold I have none but what I do have I can give: in the name of Jesus Christ, rise up and walk." And the man did. Centuries later, after all the titles had been added, a poor monk traveled to Rome and interviewed Pope Julius II, who showed him the vast riches and priceless treasures of the Church. The amazed monk was shown room after room filled with treasures of art, sculpture, jewels, gold, and silver. The proud pope said to the monk, "You see, my friend, the successor of Peter does not have to say, 'Silver and gold I have none.'" "Yes, Holy Father," replied the monk, "but by the same token, he can no longer say, 'In the name of Jesus Christ, rise up and walk.'"

That's the kind of a story that makes us ask, "Have we lost something on the way? What was it that made Peter and Paul tick?" The answer is Jesus.

For Peter, it was, "Lord, to whom shall we go? We have come to believe that you have the words of eternal life." For Paul is was, "It is no longer I who live, but Christ lives in me" and "I am determined to know nothing else but Jesus Christ and him crucified." Recalling our founding fathers reminds us that if we as the Church have fallen on hard times could it be because Jesus is no longer the center of our lives as he was for them? It's a thought, not just for the day, but for *this* day, *this* time, *this* place, *this* heart of yours and mine.

8

The Desert Fathers of Egypt

About three or four hundred years after Jesus, Mary, Joseph, Peter, and Paul, when Christianity became legal, there appeared in the deserts around Palestine and especially Egypt a group of men known as "The Desert Fathers." That they went to the desert was significant because, you recall, that's where their religion began. They went back to the sources, as it were. After all, it was in the desert that God appeared to Moses. It was in the desert that a small nomadic tribe, with no resources other than what God provided—manna and quail—not only survived but flourished and passed on its revelation and experience to the world. It was in the vast loneliness and hot cauldron of the desert that a People of God was forged.

The Desert Fathers went back to the sources because they were reacting against the laxity of the faith. Christianity had become legal and privileged by the emperor, and soon it became politic to become a Christian. Laxity set in and the cities became corrupt. There were no more "red" martyrs to inspire. It was difficult to hold onto the faith amidst such distraction. So a whole group of people opted for "white" martyrdom. They fled to the desert—these Desert Fathers—and founded monasteries as havens of renewal and spiritual refreshment. In time people would flock to them like the crowds flocked to John the Baptist, and they sat at the feet of the holy desert monk called the "Abba" or Abbot. The common refrain was, "Speak a word, Father, that we might live." And so they did. Their words, sparse and to the point, were, like John the Baptist's, totally uncompromising when it came to seeking holiness.

The Desert Fathers, like desert-dwelling John the Baptist, appeared decidedly eccentric at times, but there was a deep purpose in what they did. If, for example, they went without sleep, it was because they were practicing Advent and watching for the Lord. If they did not speak often, it was because they were listening to God. If they fasted, it was because they were fed by God's word. It was God that mattered to them, and their asceticism was only a means to that end. Eventually, their teachings, their sayings and stories were remembered, passed around, collected, meditated on. Here in this chapter, briefly, are some samplings.

Anastasius

Anastasius was abbot of a monastery in Egypt. The monastery had a large collection of books, one among them being a rare volume worth a fortune. One day a visiting monk chanced upon the book and, succumbing to temptation, walked away with it. The theft was discovered the same day and it was not hard to guess who the culprit was, but Anastasius refused to send anyone after the monk for fear that he might say he had not taken it and add the sin of perjury to that of theft. The monk meanwhile was trying to sell the book and eventually found a buyer, a rich man who asked him to leave the book with him for a day so that he could get it evaluated. When the monk had gone, the man hastened to the monastery and showed the book to Anastasius. The abbot recognized it instantly but did not say anything. "A monk wants to sell it to me," said his visitor. "He's asking for a gold sovereign. You are knowledgeable about books. Is this book worth that much'?"

"It's worth much, much more than a sovereign," said the abbot. "It's a valuable book." The man thanked the abbot and left. The next day when the monk came, the rich man informed him that he would like to buy the book and was prepared to pay the price he had mentioned. The monk was overjoyed. "Whom did you show it to?" he asked. "Anastasius, the abbot." His visitor turned pale. "And what did he say?" "He said the book was worth a sovereign." "And what else?"

"Nothing."

The monk was both amazed and touched. He realized that the abbot had refused to reclaim his lost treasure so that he, the thief would not get into trouble. Nobody had ever shown him such love; nobody had ever behaved so nobly toward him. "I've changed my mind, I don't want to sell it," he said and took the book from the man.

"I'll give you two sovereigns," said the customer. The monk walked away without answering. He went directly to the monastery and handed the book to the abbot, tears brimming in his eyes. "Keep it," said Anastasius. "When I learned you had borrowed it I decided to give it to you."

Please take it back," pleaded the monk, "but let me stay here and learn wisdom from you." His wish was granted. He spent the rest of his years in the monastery modeling his life after that of the saintly Anastasius.

John the Dwarf

John the Dwarf announced to his brother monk one day that he was going off deeper into the desert by himself to live as an angel. After several days the monk heard a knock on his door. "Who is it?" he asked. A voice, weakened by hunger, replied, "John!" The monk inside responded (with some satisfaction, I suspect), "John it can't be, for John is now an angel and has no need of food or shelter." But, after a pause, he took the humbled John in and set him to work again in a more balanced life.

St. Anthony

Once the great St. Anthony was relaxing with his disciples outside his hut when a hunter came by. The hunter was surprised and mildly shocked and rebuked Anthony for taking it easy. It was not his idea of what a monk should be doing. But Anthony said, "Bend your bow and shoot an arrow." And the hunter did so. "Bend it again and shoot another," said Anthony. And the hunter did again and again. The hunter finally said, "Abba Anthony, if I keep my bow always stretched, it will break." "So it is with the monk," replied Anthony. "If we push ourselves beyond measure we will break; it is right from time to time to relax our efforts."

Abbot Arsenius

Some monks were proposing to go to the city of Thebaid to look for some flax, and they agreed that as long as they were in the area they would look in on the famous Abba Arsenius. So a messenger came one day to the Abba and announced, "Some brothers who have come all the way from Alexandria wish to see you." The old Abba shrewdly asked why they had come and learned that they were here mainly to look for flax at Thebaid. So he told the messenger, "They will certainly not see the face of Arsenius for they have not come primarily on my account but because of their work. Make them rest and send them away in peace and tell them that the old man cannot receive them."

The Master

This one on pride: when the devil saw a seeker of truth on his way to the hut of the Abba, he was determined to do everything in his power to turn him back from his quest. So he subjected him to every form of temptation—wealth, lust, prestige—but the seeker was able to fight off these temptations quite easily. When he reached the Master's house, the seeker, however, was somewhat taken aback to see the Master sitting in an upholstered chair with his disciples at his feet. "That man certainly lacks humility, the principal virtue of saints," he thought to himself. Then he observed other things about the Master he did not like. For one thing, the Master took little notice of him. "I suppose that's because I do not fawn over him like the others do," he said to himself. He also disliked the kind of clothes the Master wore and the somewhat conceited way he spoke.

All this led him to the conclusion that he had come to the wrong place and must continue his quest elsewhere. As he walked out of the room, the Abba, who had seen the devil seated in the corner of the hut, said, "You need not have worried, tempter. He was yours from the very first, you know."

Abba Abraham and St. Mary the Harlot

Finally there is the story of Abba Abraham and his niece. Abba Abraham was a holy man and a great ascetic. He had eaten nothing but herbs and roots for fifty years. Dressed in wild camel's hair like John the Baptist, he lived simply and very austerely in total self-discipline.

It so happened one day that his only brother died and left a niece, and there was no one to care for her. So Abba Abraham, in his kindness, took her in and nourished and cherished her. She grew up to be beautiful both in body and in spirit. She followed Abba Abraham, prayed with him, and was filled with grace.

One day, a wandering monk came, as was their custom, to hear the word of God from the holy man, Abba Abraham, and was smitten by the beauty of his niece. While taking advantage of the hospitality of Abba Abraham, who was out visiting a sick monk, he was overcome by lust and raped the poor girl. She was so mortified and ashamed that in desperation she fled before Abba Abraham returned home. She fled to the city where, feeling so violated and disgraced, she became a prostitute. In vain did the distraught Abba Abraham look for his niece, until he heard one day what had happened to her and that she was plying her trade at a certain tavern.

Abba Abraham took off his simple camel's hair shirt, disguised himself as a military man with all the regalia, and went to that town. He stormed boisterously into the tavern and ordered bottles of wine and rich, red meat, and loudly downed it all to his heart's content and to the amazement of the onlookers. After he finished his dinner, he asked the innkeeper for that wench named Mary, for he said, "I have come a long way for the love of Mary!"

She was brought to him, rouged and coarse, and did not recognize this hard-eating and hard-drinking soldier. He grabbed her around the waist and twirled her around. Coquettishly she asked, "What do you want?" He shouted, "I've come a long way for the love of Mary!" And then they stopped, and he looked deeply into her eyes and said very, very softly. "I have come a long way for the love of Mary." She recognized her uncle and she wept bitterly and returned home with him. She became known as "St. Mary the Harlot" But Abba Abraham, the hermit monk, became incarnate in a hard-drinking soldier "for the love of Mary."

This is a story that tells me that no matter how far I fall, how untrue I become, how unfaithful I am, how shameless I become, how wounded, God will seek me out. He will do crazy things he's never done before. God will nag at me, pursue me, don many disguises—maybe a child, a spouse, a friend, a stranger—but he will come "for love of me."

9

St. Thérèse of Lisieux

There was a young girl named Thérèse who became known as Thérèse of Lisieux or St. Thérèse of the Child Jesus or St. Thérèse the Little Flower. She was born on January 2, 1873, the youngest of nine children. She lost her mother to breast cancer when she was four. Five of her sisters entered religious life. Her life was quiet and sheltered and devout. It was hidden. It was uneventful. It was brief. She died over a hundred years ago, in 1897, at age twenty-four.

At age fifteen, Thérèse, by special permission of the bishop, entered the Carmelite convent where two of her sisters were. She remained there till she died. Her life, as I said, was uneventful. She didn't go on any great missions, like Francis Xavier. She didn't perform any great works, like Peter Claver. In fact, when she did die in her small convent, the mother superior in charge of writing the obituary was very troubled because she confessed that she had nothing to say about her. And she asked one of the nuns there for help and all that she could say was, "Thérèse was a sweet little sister who never did anything."

And yet Thérèse became easily one of the most popular figures of the entire twentieth century, rivaling Florence Nightingale. Within twenty-five years, she was named a saint by the Church. She had terrific impact on a whole variety of people's lives. There was, for example, James Keller, a priest born and raised in Oakland, who became the founder and director of the Christopher Movement. He attributes his whole direction and vision of life to St. Thérèse. Dorothy Day, up for canonization, attributes her conversion to Saint Thérèse and wrote a biography of her. Another person who had Saint Thérèse as a favorite was Jack Keroauc, poet laureate of the Beat Generation.

So what was her legacy that captivated so many diverse people? What lesson does she have for us? The first lesson comes from the very fact of her age. She was very young. She was only fifteen when she entered the Carmelite convent. She only lived nine years longer. She died, as mentioned, at the age of twenty-four. She taught us that you don't have to be old to be holy. And she taught us that young people are equally called to the greatest of holiness.

Her second lesson came when, about three years before she died, her superior ordered her to write an autobiography. And her brief life and that small journal, called "A Story of the Soul," really revolutionized modern thinking about holiness, for she taught us what was revolutionary at the time: that every single Christian is called to holiness. We are all called to holiness, not just clergy, not just people in religious orders, not just missionaries, and not just martyrs. We are all called to great holiness.

The final lesson she taught us was that holiness could be found in the ordinary. She called her secret the "little way." She wrote, "In my 'little way' are only very ordinary things. And little souls can do everything I do…Doing one's ordinary work, our ordinary life is quite enough provided we do it with great love and great joy." And that's exactly what she did. For her, it was washing laundry and sweeping corridors and trying to stay awake at meditation time. To her, smallness and weakness made a person more of a claimant on God's attention. That's why, she wrote, "Prayer arises, if at all, from incompetence, our sense of incompleteness, that drives us to God. Grace comes as a gift, received only by those with open hands, and often failure is what causes us to open our hands."

Most of the statues, paintings, and pictures of Thérèse show her with a bouquet of roses or with roses at her feet or with a rose in her hand. The roses are a sign of her caring and loving for her community and people all over the world, for she had said, "I will send roses from heaven. I intend to spend my entire life in heaven continuing to do good work on earth." And so she has.

She kept her word as this story reveals. A lawyer was browsing in a bookstore, where he picked up the biography of Jack Kerouac and discovered, to his surprise, that Kerouac was deeply moved by the story of St. Thérèse of Lisieux and her "shower of roses." The lawyer thought, surely there is the intercession of the saints, and the shower of roses is a nice figure of speech—or is it only that? The lawyer found out in this unusual happening. He relates:

> I remember during World War II that my father, a naval surgeon, was thought to have been a casualty during an amphibious landing in the Pacific. My mother gathered the family together and began a novena to St. Thérèse. The very next day, the doorbell rang and there stood a neighbor—it was winter 1941—with a dozen long-stemmed roses. He hadn't heard that my father was missing, he knew nothing of our prayers, he just thought our family would like the flowers. Were the roses just a coincidence? Was the neighbor's gift a fluke? My mother, who shortly afterwards learned that my father was alive, believed till the end of her days that the bouquet of roses did not happen by chance. It was, as she always described it, a sign. Are these things flukes or are these things brief glimpses behind the curtain of existence reminding us that we are awaited, that we are loved?

The Little Flower was no shrinking violet. She was frail and powerful, reclusive and global, a hidden treasure, a quiet singer of subversive songs.

10

St. Catherine of Genoa and St. Joan of Oregon

Catherine of Genoa was born there in 1447. She was born into high society as we would put it. Her parents could boast of two popes in the family, Innocent IV and Adrian V. (Adrian V has the distinction of being the only pope on record who was not a priest when he was elected and who had one of the shortest reigns in papal history: he died after ruling for only a little over a month.) When Catherine was thirteen she very much wanted to join the convent, to follow her older sister, who had already done so. Her parents, however, wouldn't let her, and the convent said she was too young. That was that, and Catherine seems to have dropped the notion entirely. What she didn't know was that her parents had something else in mind for her.

There was a feud between her family and another family—the Adorno family—that they wanted to repair. Think of Shakespeare's Romeo and Juliet from the Capulet and Montague families. Thus when Catherine was fifteen, her parents arranged her marriage to Giuliano Adorno. Unfortunately, in this case, the matchmakers had given little weight to the incompatibility between Catherine and her husband. They couldn't have been more different, and it was a marriage made in hell. While Catherine was modest and devout, her husband, in the words of her biographer, "was entirely the opposite in his mode of life." That tame phrase means that he was a compulsive gambler, a spendthrift, and unceasingly unfaithful. Understandably, Catherine quickly sank into a state of depression that lasted for the first five years of what was to be a childless marriage.

For another five years Catherine tried to pull herself out of this depression by going in the opposite direction and throwing herself into the frivolous diversions of high society. But this only left her feeling sadder and emptier. Finally, at the age of twenty-five, she uttered a desperate prayer for some relief from the torment of her existence, even praying for an illness that would confine her to bed. But a turning point was at hand. One day in 1473, while kneeling for confession, she had a mystical experience. She was suddenly overcome with remorse for the mediocrity of her life and at the same time with an overwhelming sense of God's goodness and mercy. "No more world," she was heard to utter. "No more sins." She resolved to let go of all the carefully hoarded resentments that had cramped her spirit. From that moment, by all accounts, she began to live a new life.

The first thing Catherine did was to go to work at the local hospital—hardly ordinary behavior for a woman of her social standing. She began with washing patients and cleaning their bedpans. No job was too repugnant. The miracle, though, was that as she grew in the practice of love, living no longer for herself alone, she also found herself growing in her capacity for happiness. Around this time, as it happened, her husband's free-spending ways finally caught up with him. The couple was reduced to bankruptcy. They were forced to give up their grand mansion and move into a simple cottage, much more to Catherine's liking. Eventually, in part through her example, her husband reformed his own life, even becoming a lay Franciscan. They moved into an apartment in the hospital, where, after many years of work Catherine assumed the job of director.

Catherine remained a laywoman throughout her life, even after her husband's death. She attracted a wide circle of spiritual followers, drawn not only by the opportunity to work alongside her but also by the chance to benefit from her wisdom. In her final years, under the guidance of a new spiritual director, she wrote several spiritual treatises and often experienced mystical ecstasies. It was said that she conversed with angels. She died in Genoa in 1510, at age sixty-three. After her death a book about her and her writings were published. She was beatified in 1675 and canonized in 1737.

Catherine surely qualifies for the niche of the patroness of lousy marriages. Anyone who has been forced into a marriage of convenience, who has been married to an insensitive and unfaithful spouse, can relate to her. Her response to this situation is worth following: move, not inward to despair and self-pity, but outward toward works of compassion and caring.

In the sense of clinging firmly to Christ in times of tragedy Catherine readily evokes another woman, wife, and mother from six centuries later, a woman hurt deeply, not by her husband, but by her parish priest. It is the twentieth century, a time of the exposure of the Church's worse gaping wound, the clergy sexual abuse scandal. The woman's name is Joan Ryan and she tells her poignant story.

> My son Peter became an altar boy when he was ten years old. The abuse began before he had ever finished his training. Father Maurice Grammond told Peter that he would be killed if he told anyone. Even though complaints of abuse had been received by the Archdiocese from outraged parents in Fr. Grammond's previous assignments, he was moved along yet again, this time to our parish in Seaside in Oregon.
>
> Peter soon fell into depression. He quit school sports, was expelled in his freshman year of high school for smoking marijuana. He began a cycle of drug and alcohol abuse and eventually rehabilitation

followed by still more substance abuse. Peter repressed these memories of his abuse until an adult.

I couldn't heal my child and after more than thirty years of quiet lonely suffering, the floodgates of memories opened up and quickly overwhelmed Peter. He shot himself to death and we buried him this past March at St. Ignatius church in Oregon.

Like so many others, she could have, justifiably, turned her back on the Church. Instead, in the spirit of Catherine, she adds these words: "I still cling to my faith, and I'm still active in two parishes. I'm doing all I can to transform the memory of my son from one of tragedy to one of nobility. I want his and other victims' deaths not to be in vain, but instead to become a healing point for our broken Church. I want good to come of Peter's sad death."

Two noble saints.

11

St. Callixtus of Rome and St. John of London

Many people who have visited Rome have made sure that they saw one of its most popular sites, the intriguing catacombs of Pope St. Callixtus. How did it get that name? The answer involves a fascinating but murky character called Callixtus. We're not sure of what we know about him because most of our knowledge comes from his bitter enemies, and that tells us not only the obvious fact that Callixtus wasn't always a pope but that he was once a slave. He wasn't always a saint. On the contrary, he started out as a first-class embezzler, cheat, con man, and fraud.

His story, as it is given, goes like this. In the early third century a man named Carpophorus set up a bank for his fellow Christians, particularly widows, who needed a safe place to keep their limited funds. Now, Carpophorus happened to have a slave named Callixtus who had some talent in managing money, so Carpophorus put him in charge of the widows' fund. Well, when auditing time came, it turned out that Callixtus had made some very bad investments, including investing some of the money right into his own pocket.

For this bit of financial sleight of hand Carpophorus sent him to jail to do hard labor. But eventually the ruined depositors prevailed on Carpophorus to release Callixtus in the hope that the wily man might recover some of the pilfered money. After all, the man was a genius with money. The first thing the newly freed and over-eager Callixtus did was to barge in on a Jewish religious service one Saturday trying to get back some of the funds from Jewish investors. A brawl ensued, and Callixtus was nabbed once more, and this time he was sent to do hard labor in the salt mines on the island of Sardinia. That should have been the end of him. But somehow he conned his guards to let him sneak out with some visitors, and so he escaped. At the same time, however, it did seem that prison life had tempered the man, and time in the salt mines had turned him around. He genuinely seemed to be repentant of his former life.

Carpophorus on the other hand was not at all convinced of Callixtus' spiritual turnaround, and still saw his former slave as a low-life sinner. Thus Carpophorus was duly scandalized when a kindly priest named Zephryrinus took Callixtus in and offered him acceptance and forgiveness. (The true story, it was rumored, was that Callixtus bribed the ignorant and illiterate priest.) Eventually, when he became pope, Zephrynius not only ordained Callixtus a deacon, but he put him in charge of a Christian cemetery on the Appian Way—the famed catacomb now known as the catacomb of St. Callixtus.

There's more to this story: when Zephryninus died, the Roman clergy turned around and elected Callixtus pope! But new accusations soon followed Callixtus. It was said that he allowed all repentant sinners absolution (apostates, murderers, and adulterers were excluded), allowed bishops to be married more than once, live-in couples to be treated as married, and so on. All this seems to be false. The new pope became the official patron of the famed church of St. Mary in Trastevere, about which apocryphal lore had said that it was built on the site of a tavern because the emperor felt that the worship of any god was preferable to a tavern.

Pope Callixtus I died a martyr around the year 223. Legend says he was thrown into the well in the church he built. Whatever we can salvage about this man, we know that he represents the classic journey of going from spiritual rags to spiritual riches—slave to cheat to con man to repentant sinner to pope to saint.

That gives us hope. And it's a hope that is played out through the ages. To bring the reader up to date, I think of John Profumo. Those who lived in the 1960s might remember the name. It was all over the newspapers. And why not? Intrigue, politics, sex— the media could not let it alone. Here's the story: John Profumo was the former Minister of War for Great Britain during the time of the Cold War. His downfall began on the grounds of a grand English country estate when he watched a beautiful young woman emerge from a swimming pool. He asked who she was. He was told that her name was Christine Keeler, a prominent English call girl. Profumo was so smitten with the young woman that he began a secret relationship with her. Unknown to him, however, she was also having an affair at the same time with the Soviet naval attaché in London—a member of the KGB. When the story finally broke and Profumo's part in the whole affair was exposed, it became the most sensational sex scandal of the era.

Then, as scandals go, it slowly withered away giving place to the next one. The press was no longer interested in John Profumo. But we are. He retired from the government but, unlike today, he did not appear on the talk show circuit, sell his story to the National Enquirer, or seek an advance for a tell-all best seller. He understood how his recklessness had brought embarrassment to his wife and country. Not long afterward he contacted Toynbee Hall, a charitable mission in the East End of London, and asked whether they needed help. This blue-blooded British aristocrat and long-standing member of Parliament started washing dishes and helping with the children's playgroup. He would remain there for the next forty years. He disappeared amid the grimy tenements of east London and did good works till he died.

Two journeys, two sinners, two saints.

12

St. Peter Claver of Spain

Long an institution, slavery, in Europe at least, died out over time so that by the twelfth century it was virtually unknown. Then in the fifteenth century, European exploration and exploitation of Africa, Asia, and the Americas revived the slave trade with a vengeance. As one of the first new lands colonized by the Portuguese, the Canary Islands became the first place where slavery was reintroduced. When word of this reached Pope Eugenius IV in 1435, he fired off a letter to the local bishop denouncing the enslavement of the Canary Islanders and demanding that the enslaved be set free. His plea fell on deaf ears as the Portuguese and then the Spanish pushed farther and farther into fabulously wealthy lands. The temptation to exploit the riches of these territories through the slave labor of the local population became irresistible. Besides, the explorers argued, those American Indians, Africans, and Asians were clearly less than human, quite inferior, brutish, primitive beings.

In spite of papal condemnations, greed won out, and the international slave trade flourished among Catholics and Protestants for another four hundred years—and often as not with the cooperation of some native African blacks who grew rich by rounding up and selling their fellow countrymen and women.

Into this context a son, Peter, was born to the Clavers, a farming family from the province of Catalonia in Spain. Peter was a bright, religious lad, but, like Hamlet, he grew up finding it very hard ever to make a decision and stick with it. His parents eventually sent Peter to a school run by the new order of Jesuits in Barcelona. The active, exciting, and varied life of the Jesuits appealed to Peter. He talked a lot about joining but typically could never quite commit himself. Finally, after vacillating for several years, Peter Claver asked to be received as a Jesuit novice. True to form, he had barely entered the novitiate when he began to second-guess himself. What if he was not cut out for an active life as a missionary or parish priest? Maybe this, maybe that.

Fortunately, help was nearby in the person of the college doorkeeper (doorkeepers seem to figure a lot in the lives of the saints), a seventy-two-year-old lay brother named Alphonsus Rodriguez. Brother Alphonsus had had a family and a career, but after his wife and children all died, he gave up his business and entered the religious life. Although he was a Jesuit brother now, he hadn't lost his knack for handling a tough customer who couldn't decide what he wanted. So it was he who assured Peter that he did indeed belong with the Jesuits and, moreover, that Peter should ask his superiors to send him to the Americas as a missionary. Peter was taken aback by this but eventually summoned up the courage to ask his superiors to assign him to the American mission. They finally gave their consent and sent him to Cartagena, Colombia, as an unordained novice.

Cartagena's location on the Caribbean Sea made it one of the principal ports for the slave trade in the New World: twelve thousand enslaved Africans were unloaded in Cartagena every year. You can imagine that, after weeks crammed together in the dark holds of the slave ships, these tragic people were filthy, weak from hunger and dehydration, and half mad with fear. Many were sick. Some were dying. They were driven like cattle into holding pens near the dock to be sorted out and sold. The only white man who treated the Africans kindly was a Jesuit priest, Father Alphonse de Sandoval.

When Peter Claver, the apprehensive new Jesuit novice from Spain, arrived in Cartagena, Father de Sandoval made him his assistant. This turned out to be the turning point for Peter. The work in the slave pen transformed him. Once he recognized that he could do something for God and his fellow human beings, all doubts, all qualms, all uncertainties vanished. Now every time a slaver sailed into Cartagena's harbor, Peter took the pilot's boat out to the ship and began his work at once down in the hold. On shore, as sailors and soldiers herded the slaves into the pens, Peter went with them. Through his interpreters Peter tried to comfort the Africans and learn what they needed. Every day Peter and his interpreters returned with more food, more water, more medicines, and as he treated the Africans, he explained to them the basics of the Catholic faith. It is said that during the forty-four years Father

Claver served in the slave pens, he baptized over one hundred thousand Africans. Whatever the number of converts there may have been, Peter regarded them as his parishioners. He kept up a steady round of visitations, saying Mass for his converts, bringing them the sacraments, and continuing their religious instruction.

In time Peter Claver's devotion to his African converts enraged the white population of Cartagena. The charges: he was keeping slaves from their work. He was contaminating churches and chapels with his congregations of unwashed Africans. He was profaning the Blessed Sacrament by giving Communion to these "animals." Some well-born ladies even refused to enter a church if Father Claver had said Mass there for slaves. Even some of Peter's brother Jesuits thought he was excessively devoted to the Africans. No matter. After years of wavering Peter Claver had found his vocation, and he would not be deterred from it.

Peter kept up his exhausting routine until, one day, when he was seventy-four years old, he collapsed in the slave pen. Taken back to the Jesuit residence, Peter lay on his deathbed, abandoned by the white Christians of Cartagena. The only one who nursed the dying man was an African servant. The end came quickly. Late in the evening on September 7, 1654, Peter Claver received the last sacraments, then fell unconscious and died shortly after midnight. A crowd of slaves broke down the gates of the Jesuit residence so they could see their saint one last time.

Fast forward: on January 15, 1888, the people of Rome witnessed a double canonization as Pope Leo XIII declared that Peter Claver and Alphonsus Rodriguez were saints.

Peter Claver is a good patron saint not only for the enslaved everywhere but also for those who have trouble making up their minds.

13

St. Catherine of Siena

You can't understand fourteenth-century Catherine of Siena apart from the tumultuous times in which she lived: a time of the Black Death, the Avignon Captivity of the popes (meaning that the papacy had moved from Rome to Avignon in France), and the Great Schism (meaning that at one time there were three rival popes and papacies). That's enough turmoil for a hundred lifetimes. She was born as a twin in 1347—the twenty-third child—and her house still exists in Siena. Her mother ultimately had twenty-five children, many of whom died. Her twin sister was handed over to a wet nurse and soon died. Catherine was nursed by her mother and thrived.

Catherine was said to have visions early on. When one of her older married sisters died, she was told to marry her brother-in-law but she refused and retreated into fasting. When she was sixteen she joined the Dominican associates and lived in a little room in her father's house and promptly distressed her family by giving away much of the family's food and possessions. In 1366, she experienced what she called a "mystical marriage" to Jesus and left her house hermitage to enter the public life of service where she helped the sick, the poor, and prisoners, and walked with the condemned to the gallows. Her ministry was especially important because the Black Death, which greeted Catherine when she was born, returned in force in 1374.

Apparently a woman of great personal charisma and charm, she began to attract followers even while provoking the displeasure and persecution of some of the Dominican friars and nuns. At this time she began to write letters to many people, and hers was eventually a huge correspondence. Actually, being unable to write herself, she dictated her letters. She corresponded with officials, princes, and popes. She was often asked for advice. She took it upon herself to implore Pope Gregory XI to leave Avignon and return to Rome. She urged the reform of the clergy and chastised the pope for arming the Tuscans but, inconsistently, she also promoted another crusade. She entered into the politics of public life—always dangerous in medieval times—and escaped an attempt on her life. When the Great Schism broke out (three popes simultaneously) she backed the Roman claimant, Urban VI, who summoned her to Rome in 1378, and there she was to remain until her death in 1380, at age thirty-three. Her mother, having lost most of her children and grandchildren, lived to eighty-nine.

Catherine's letters—more than 300 have survived—are considered a highpoint of Tuscan literature. They are often forthright as when she wrote to some cardinals who were supporting the antipope, "What made you do this? You are flowers who shed no perfume, but stench that makes the whole world reek." Writing to Gregory XI, she said, "Be not a timorous child, but manly…" She was practical. Asked by one of her nuns, "How can I pay God back for all of his goodness to me? How can I give back to God some glory for all of God's kind compassion, mercy, and generosity?" St. Catherine answered, "It won't do you any good to do any more penances. It won't do much good to build a great church. It won't do you much good to add more quiet time in prayer. But I'll tell you something you can do to really pay God back for the compassion God gives you. Find someone as unlovable as you are and give that person the kind of love that God has given you."

Catherine's piety was couched in florid medieval terms that would put many people off today, for example, her fixation on the blood of Jesus ("I…long to see you drowned and transformed in his overflowing blood.") Miracle stories about her are typically exaggerated. Still, her mystical visions have inspired many and she has become the unofficial patron saint of church reform. She was canonized in 1461, and in May of 1940 Pope Pius XII made her a joint patron saint of Italy, along with St. Francis of Assisi. Later, Pope Paul VI gave her the title of Doctor of the Church. In 1990, Pope John Paul II made her one of Europe's patron saints.

Her head is on display in the church of San Domenico in Siena as well as her thumb. The rest of her body rests in Rome in the Dominican church of Santa Maria sopra Minerva near the house where she died. Mystic, activist, adviser to popes, reformer, doctor of the Church, servant of the poor—these are some of the attributes of a remarkable woman, St. Catherine of Siena.

AMERICAN
SAINTS

14

Rose Hawthorne

Catholics publicly celebrate some stellar saints in their liturgical world: St. Alphonsus, founder of the Redemptorists. St. Dominic, founder of the Dominicans, St. Lawrence, St. Maximilian Kolbe, St. Bernard, St. Pius X, St. Bartolomew, St. Monica, St. Augustine— all heavy hitters. But, as we noted, there are the underground saints, among whom is this as yet uncanonized saint (her cause is being considered), an ordinary spiritual star who was married, though not happily or, unfortunately, lastingly. She happened to carry a celebrity name before celebrities were invented. Her name is Rose Hawthorne, and she was the daughter of the very famous American author, Nathaniel Hawthorne. Remember, he wrote *The House of the Seven Gables* and *The Scarlet Letter*.

Her story, briefly, goes like this. At age twenty, Rose met a young American writer in Europe and married him. They had one son together who died of diphtheria at the age of four. And her husband, throughout their marriage, was a confirmed alcoholic. After twenty years of very difficult married life, both of them, in 1891, were converted to the Catholic Church and became very prominent and active Catholics. While their conversion may have been good for their faith life, it didn't do anything special for their marriage. It foundered. They separated. Three years later, their separation was permanent.

Rose was now in her early forties. After a life devoted to her husband and to society events, social events, and entertaining in high society in New England and New York, she began to look for meaning and service to give value to her days and nights. And she found it in a very surprising and even frightening place. She found meaning and service among victims of cancer in the poorest slums of New York City. Today, cancer still frightens us. But, in 1890, it was considered and viewed, not just as incurable, but also as contagious. The moment a patient in a hospital was diagnosed with cancer, they were moved out and barred from entry to any other hospital in the city. If you had a lot of wealth, your family could take care of you. Otherwise, you were exiled onto an island in the middle of the East River, or you gathered with other cancer patients in the slums.

Rose took a three-month course in nursing, rented a three-room tenement apartment in the very tough, lower East Side of New York, and began visiting cancer patients, tenement by tenement. She wrote about some of the things she did on a typical day, for example: on one day in October, 1896, she fed and clothed a starving mother and daughter; she changed the dressings for a cancer patient two times; she visited an elderly woman dying of cancer; she prevented the eviction by a landlord of a tenant because he had cancer; and she brought food to a child dying of meningitis.

Before long, she was inviting the patients into her three little rooms, into her apartment. She spent day after day washing the cancerous sores and changing the bedclothes of her impoverished guests. But even more important, she was determined to offer friendship and respect and a sense of worth and a sense of value to those whom others considered outcasts. She drew a motto from the writing of St. Vincent de Paul: "I am for God and the poor." She rented a larger building and named it "St. Rose's Free Home for Incurable Cancer." She set two rules for those who wanted to work with her. If you worked with her, you had to live with the poor and accept no salary. And the second rule was that you would accept no payment ever from a patient or from their family or from the state. She expanded her work and she funded more buildings by begging from her acquaintances and friends in society, and by advertising in the New York papers. One of her most generous and constant benefactors was Mark Twain.

In 1900, she and her helpers joined a community of women religious Dominicans. But after six years with them she left and founded her own community, which she named "The Servants for the Relief of Incurable Cancer." She died in 1926, at the age of seventy-five, and today her community continues her work. They are usually referred to as the "Hawthorne Dominicans." And they continue to be faithful to Rose Hawthorne, serving the poor and refusing to accept any payment from families or from the government. Her engagement ring and wedding ring are exactly where she left them, on the hand of a statue of Jesus in one of the principal buildings that they staff in New York.

What lessons do we learn from Rose Hawthorne? The first one has to be about marriage. Just because a marriage doesn't work out, or because our family is dysfunctional, it doesn't mean that our life doesn't work out and that we have to be dysfunctional. It means that we can begin again and find a new life.

Second, we learn once more that there is so much hidden love going on all the time, that quiet holiness is widespread and persistent. Rose's life reminds us again that there is a tremendous amount of good being done in very secret ways every day by anonymous people. The saintly underground flourishes.

The third thing is about the poor. The American bishops said that the test of a healthy country, the test of a healthy society, is not how high its standard of living is or how well off the well off are. The test of a healthy country is how it treats its poorest and weakest citizens. A test for Christians, for those who try to follow the gospel is, how do we stand with the poor, the needy, the sick?

Rose Hawthorne's life challenges us to look beyond scandal, terrorism, hurt, and disappointment, to minister to all of God's children.

15

Barney Casey

Born in 1870 in Wisconsin, Barney Casey came from one of those large immigrant Irish families that we can't even imagine today. He was the sixth out of sixteen children, ten boys and six girls. He was a fairly non-descript kid, a teenager who was a mainstay of his family and worked the family farm. Early on he had contracted diphtheria, which damaged his voice, leaving it somewhat wispy. He eventually moved on to find work where he could as a lumberjack, brick maker, prison guard, and finally a streetcar conductor. One day he witnessed a tragedy that set him on a new course in life. It happened this way.

On a cold rainy afternoon as he guided his streetcar around a curve in a rough part of town, he saw a crowd of people gathered on the tracks. He stopped the car, pushed through the crowd to see a young drunken sailor standing over a woman he had assaulted and stabbed repeatedly. He couldn't get the brutal incident out of his mind. He prayed for the sailor, he prayed for the woman, and gradually he felt he must pray for the whole world.

So at age twenty-one he quit his job and applied to St. Francis Seminary in Milwaukee. Five years later Barney applied to and joined the Capuchin order at St. Bonaventure's in Detroit, where he got his religious name of Solanus—Solanus Casey—after St.

Francis Solanus. But Barney was not very bright. Or at least he appeared that way because the classes were conducted in German, which he didn't know. Some seminary professors opposed his ordination, but an old priest spoke up for him, and he was ordained in 1904, at age thirty-three. Doubts about the intelligence and abilities of this underachiever still lingered, however, so the seminary would permit his ordination under one condition: that he would remain what is called a "simplex priest." That is, he could celebrate Mass but that's all. He could not hear confessions, preach, or wear the Capuchin hood. Still, although he could not preach an official sermon, he could and did give little conferences and inspirational talks, and they inspired and captivated many,

So for forty-three years Father Solanus Casey never heard a confession or gave a retreat or preached a mission. What did he do? Officially he was assigned as sacristan and lowly doorkeeper, answering the door and greeting visitors, a no-brainer. He spent his first fifteen years answering the door in Yonkers and Manhattan, and then in 1921, was transferred to Our Lady of the Angels in Harlem.

But in this desert of the ordinary, the word of God bypassed the local bishop and the chancery officials and the abbot and came to Barney, because the ordinary people were discovering something about this doorkeeper. This simple doorkeeper, having listened so intently to the word of God, turned out to be a wonderful listener to them and an insightful counselor. He had that kind of demeanor, that kind of spiritual simplicity that invited people to open their hearts to him. He became known for his great compassion and insight. Word spread, and soon many would come, bypass the prior and abbot, and ask to speak with the doorkeeper, Father Solanus.

But that wasn't all. Father Solanus was also put in charge of the Capuchin Prayer Association, and no sooner did he take charge than miracles began to happen. People were being healed of all sorts of ailments—pneumonia, heart disease, blindness. This doorkeeper also turned out to be a wonder worker. His superiors soon transferred him back to St. Bonaventure's in Detroit, where they could keep an eye and a lid on him. But there he attracted an even larger following, and so for the next two decades people trekked literally from all over the world, like the crowds that came to John in the desert, to receive the simple doorkeeper's ministry and hear his words.

Father Solanus—Barney Casey—worked twelve hours a day helping and counseling others. At night he was found praying in the chapel and often sound asleep before the altar. He became ill in his old age, and his last conscious act was to sit up in bed saying, "I give my soul to Jesus Christ." This streetcar driver turned simple priest, not trusted with anything important, died at age eighty-six on July 31, 1957. Some 20,000 people passed by his coffin. His cause is now up for canonization, and he has been declared "venerable" in the four-step process of Servants of God, Venerable, Beatified, and Saint.

Who would have thought, in the car capital of the world, the word of God would come to somebody who answers the door and a light would be let out?

16

Harriet Tubman

Her avocation was rescuing slaves along the Underground Railroad during the Civil War. She was a most unlikely leader. Her name is Harriet Tubman.

She was born at the same time (around 1822) and place in Dorchester County on the Eastern shore of Maryland as the famous ex-slave and abolitionist, Frederick Douglass. Her name was Araminta ("Minty" they called her) Ross, one of eleven slave children. As a slave she was not permitted an education—slaveholders did not want their slaves to know how to read or write and so learn about the law—and so she remained illiterate all her life. Early on she saw her two older sisters being carried off in a chain gang to work in the cotton fields in the deep South. She never forgot that.

She herself was small and frail and not considered labor material. At six she was hired out to clean a house and care for a baby and was whipped if she failed at her tasks or slackened in her duties. She soon became ill under such treatment and was sent back home as an unsuitable slave. There, nursed back to health, she absorbed a deep faith in God from her mother. From her she learned the biblical story of Moses and the Exodus, and it stayed with her as a guiding light, so much so that later in her life she would become known as the female Moses. Recovered, she was hired out to others, ran away from cruelty, was caught and whipped. By age twelve she was considered quite unemployable and was sent out to work in the fields.

As a teenager she was near a man who was going to beat his slave. The slave bolted, and the angry master picked up a two-pound weight to throw at the fleeing slave but it hit Minty by mistake. It broke her skull. The aftermath left a deep indentation in her forehead and a life-long bout of headaches, seizures, and sleeping spells giving people the impression that she was dimwitted, which was far from the truth.

In her early twenties Minty was cutting and hauling lumber with her father. While there she not only became strong physically through the hard outdoor work but also had the chance to hear about a network of slaves who were always plotting a way to freedom. In 1844, Minty married a free black man, John Tubman and changed her name to Harriet in honor of her mother. Two years later she became very ill but eventually recovered, using this enforced time to grow deeper in prayer. Then her master died, and she and the other slaves were fearful that they were going to be deported to the deep South. She and her two brothers decided to run away, and in the fall of 1849 the three fled into the woods and swamps knowing full well that bounty hunters would be hot on their trail and that severe punishments awaited them if they were caught. Her brothers lost heart and turned back, but Harriet was determined to find freedom. She finally made it to one of the network houses that one day would be known as part of the Underground Railroad. The Underground Railroad was made up of whites and blacks who took great risks. This illegal network spread westward as far as Illinois and Wisconsin and northward to Philadelphia and Boston and even to Canada.

Harriet fled from network house to network house. By this time slave owners were becoming fearful of a slave uprising where black slaves would kill white people, and several uprisings had occurred in New York and South Carolina. The most famous or notorious was that of Nat Turner, whose followers went from house to house hacking white families to death. Turner became a horror to the whites and a hero to the blacks. Fear and distrust were in the air. Repercussions and lynchings were common.

Harriet fled to Delaware and then to Pennsylvania and finally to Philadelphia, which provided a haven for runaways. She now felt free, though sad that her brothers were not with her. She knew in her heart that she would have to go back and rescue them. "I was free," she said, "and they should be free." In Philadelphia she had to face poverty, racial prejudice, the fear of kidnapping by slave catchers, and the reach of the new 1850 Fugitive Slave Act, which could have sent her back to Maryland. Nevertheless she could mingle with the many former slaves there, walk freely in the parks, attend church, and take part in discussions. She got a job as a domestic and saved her money. Eventually she became deeply interested in politics and attended abolitionist and women's rights meetings.

But Harriet was still homesick and, as we said, desirous of freeing her family and other slaves. She began learning the ins and outs of the Underground Railroad, learning the names of key people and places, and finally she made the decision to take on the role of a female "abductor," that is, one who would go back South and seek out fugitives. She began with her niece and her children who were about to be shipped to the South. She met them in Baltimore and led them to freedom to Pennsylvania. Next she rescued her brother and his family and then, at last, at enormous personal risk, decided to save her beloved husband. She bought him a new suit and secretly sent him word that she was about to rescue him from slavery. She was shocked and dismayed when he sent back word that he did not want to be rescued. He had remarried, and he did not want to see her! She was furious but ultimately decided to go on with her life. This decision was made easier by her profound sense that she had been called by God to free others. She eventually wound up freeing her other brothers and her parents. Using the Wilmington, Delaware, house of a Quaker abolitionist as a checkpoint, from 1850 to 1860 she conducted between eleven and thirteen escape missions. Since the Fugitive Slave act many slaves, in fear of recapture, were fleeing to Canada. Harriet brought many of them to Ontario, her base of operation from 1851 to 1857.

Thus began an adventurous and risky life, and Harriet became like someone out of a James Bond movie. She carried forged passports, often traveled in exotic disguises, and had prearranged signals she was nearby, such as singing negro spirituals. She had to traverse treacherous swamps and dodge bounty hunters. She carried a gun, arranged carts with false bottoms, and tapped into secret network homes. She had an intuitive sense of reading travel directions from the stars and woods. Most of all, she clung to that biblical sense of being another Moses led by God's unseen presence. She once told an interviewer, "Now how do you suppose he wanted me to do this just for a day or a week? No! The Lord who told me to take care of my people meant me to do it just so long as I live, and so I do what he told me to do." She had many close calls. She soon became a legend much admired by the big-name abolition leaders such as William Seward, William Lloyd Garrison, Frederick Douglass, and John Brown but hated by the slaveholders who offered a $40,000 reward for her capture. In 1858, the anti-slavery Senator William Seward sold Harriet a house in Auburn, New York.

Although others were wary of John Brown's violent ways, Harriet supported him because he was a white man taking up the cause of the blacks. His ill planned and ill-fated assault at Harper's Ferry in 1859 failed and he was captured and hanged. Harriet had planned to be there but was prevented by illness. Brown's moving letters from prison and his dignity as he was led to the gallows and the fact that he had died for a cause provoked sympathy and they affected Harriet, who late in life called him "my dearest friend." Soon, however, she sensed that the Underground Railroad was becoming passé and that she would have to work for the larger issue of total emancipation. The Civil War and President Abraham Lincoln would eventually take up that issue. Harriet did not at first warm up to Lincoln and she objected to the lower pay of black soldiers.

During the war Harriet was called from her comfortable home in Auburn to work with displaced slaves who were fugitives from the South Carolina Union battle victories and had been settled by the thousands in Union camps. Harriet was overwhelmed with the task but she comforted and nursed these slaves. She also doubled as a spy and a scout finding out the positions of the Confederate troops. She even became the first women to command an armed military raid when she guided Colonel James Montgomery and his 2nd South Carolina black regiment up the Combahee River to rout the Confederate outposts where they destroyed stockpiles of weapons and liberated over 700 slaves. Later, after the Emancipation Proclamation in 1863 and after the war, she worked long hours as a hospital nurse for wounded soldiers.

The Thirteenth Amendment was passed in 1865, giving blacks citizenship and the right to vote. Harriet went back home knowing that slavery had been ended but not discrimination. She experienced that personally when the train conductor would not accept her military pass and ordered her to go the smoking car. She refused and the conductor and several others forcefully dragged her there injuring her arms and shoulder. She made it back home to Auburn penniless, applied for a pension, and was denied. She was reduced to living from hand to mouth—her neighbors would leave food on her porch—and yet still helped channel donations to the needy, and she began to plan a home for needy black people.

In 1869, her husband having been gunned down in Maryland, she married a man twenty years her junior. He died nineteen years later. Meanwhile a congressional bill granting Harriet compensation for her brave service during the war passed the House but was defeated in the Senate. Harriet continued to speak at various functions promoting women's rights. Finally by 1911 Harriet began to slow down and became very ill in 1913. This frail little slave girl with the dented head and brave heart died at age ninety-one on March 10 of that year—the same year Rosa Parks was born. She was buried in Fort Hill Cemetery in Auburn with military honors. In due time, after much neglect, the government issued a commemorative stamp of her in 1995. Currently a bill is before Congress seeking to create The Harriet Tubman Historical Park at Auburn and in Maryland.

William Seward summed up her incredible life well. "The cause of freedom owes her much; the country owes her much." Jesus summed it up better. "Blessed are those who hunger and thirst after justice. The kingdom of God is theirs."

17

Thomas Merton

Thomas Merton, a complex man—poet, mystic, monk, artist, peace activist, priest, spiritual master, ecumenist, Zen practitioner—was a man of contradictions. Jesuit writer Jim Martin tells why: Merton was a man in love with the world around him who chooses to become a cloistered monk, a trappist, Fr. M. Louis, OCSO (for the Order of Cistercians of the Strict Observance). He was an inveterate traveler who took a vow of stability, choosing to remain at the Abbey of Our Lady of Gethsemani, in the secluded hills of Kentucky. A man who freely took a vow of obedience but who spent much of his religious life butting heads with his order's superiors. A man in love with his vocation but constantly questioned it. A devout Catholic convert who was fascinated by Eastern religions. A famous writer who professed to hate (or tried to convince himself that he hated) the trappings and ''business" of fame. A man who could write one day of his desire never to write another sentence, only to write a few days later of his joy in seeing another of his books published. (In one memorable journal entry, he reveals a barely hidden satisfaction that the burlap covering his new book is the same fabric used in the chic Manhattan supper clubs of the day.)

Thomas Merton was one of the great figures of twentieth-century Catholicism. His 1948 memoir, *The Seven Storey Mountain*, which details his journey to the Trappist monastery, was a publishing phenomenon. It was a best-seller for months and months— although the New York Times would not list it because it dealt with religion. It introduced contemplative prayer to millions of readers and renewed interest in monastic life.

Who was he? What was his journey? Tom Merton was born on January 31, 1915, in a small town in the French Pyrenees. His father, Owen, a New Zealander, was a painter of some renown. Ruth, Merton's American-born mother, was also something of an artist. His parents met while studying at a studio in Paris. Merton grew up loving everything French, and in many ways France would always represent home for a rootless young Merton.

I say rootless because for most of his early life Thomas Merton found himself without a real home. Tom's mother died when he was six. Thereafter his father moved the family from place to place, town to town, and country to country while he pursued his artistic career. For a time the family (which included Tom's younger brother, John Paul) lived with his mother's family in Douglaston, New York, and then, for a while, in Bermuda. During their stay in Bermuda, his father, Owen, hoping to sell some of his paintings in New York, casually left Tom in the care of a woman author he had just met. After this, Tom, Owen, and John Paul returned to France, where Tom enrolled in a nearby secondary school.

One summer, while his father was traveling once again, Merton boarded with the Privats, a Catholic family in Murat. Here Tom was moved by the affection shown him by this elderly couple and their young nephew, who became his friend. Passages in his autobiography describing his stay with the Privats are among the tenderest he ever set down on paper. "I owe many graces to their prayers," he writes, "and perhaps ultimately the grace of my conversion and even of my religious vocation. Who shall say? But one day I shall know, and it is good to be able to be confident that I will see them again and be able to thank them."

In 1929, Merton was sent off to a boarding school in Rutland, England. He hated it. Around this time, his father fell ill, suffering from the effects of a brain tumor. Owen died in 1931, a few days before Tom's sixteenth birthday. A bright and articulate young man, Merton won a scholarship to Clare College at Cambridge, and began his university studies. It proved to be an even less congenial place for Merton than the previous school. Tom spent much of his day carousing with a bunch of hip characters. He also fathered a child. Many years later, when Merton was about to enter the Trappists, his guardian undertook an unsuccessful search for the woman and her child. The mother and child, it seems, were killed in the Blitz during the Second World War. This incident was censored out of his autobiography. Later biographers would provide a fuller account of this difficult chapter in Merton's life.

His life was lonely and aimless. He suffered separation from his only brother, missed his parents deeply, and behaved in ways that disgusted him—drinking, smoking, partying, and always showing off. Tom seemed forever to be searching for something, while remaining unaware of what he was searching for. Finally, after considering Tom's experiences in England, Tom's guardian suggested that he return to the States to continue his education. Merton was happy to accept this advice.

Columbia University and New York City proved much more agreeable to Merton. He met many companionable young men who remained his friends for life. He found his studies enjoyable. Tom also came under the influence of the popular English professor Mark Van Doren, whom Merton deeply admired for his sense of "vocation," and his "profoundly scholastic" mind. His autobiography made it clear that Merton cut a wide and wild figure at Columbia. Still, quietly, a lot was going on inside of Merton, a slow and subtle process of conversion from an old way of life to a new one.

This spiritual turnabout unfolded slowly in various ways. His study, his love of art widened his soul. His warm relationship with people like the devout Privats showed him what lived faith was like. His stolen prayers in a church in Rome, his moments beside the bed of his dying grandfather when he felt the urge to fall to his knees and pray—all added their influence. By and by he began to attend Mass at a nearby church. A few pages later in his autobiography, he was baptized as a Roman Catholic at Corpus Christi Church near Columbia University.

His life changed even more rapidly and decisively in the years after his baptism. After Columbia he began working on a master's degree in English. He also began considering a vocation to the priesthood. He quickly ran through a number of religious orders, Only the Rule of St. Francis of Assisi appealed to Tom. Providentially, a friend of his was familiar with the Franciscans at St. Bonaventure College in Olean, a town in upstate New York. So after finishing his master's degree at Columbia, Tom took a teaching position at the college. In November 1939 he applied to enter the Franciscans but his application was rejected. One of Merton's biographers conjectures that Merton's rejection by the Franciscans might have stemmed from several factors: Merton's fathering of a child, being a new convert, and perhaps "his sense of his own unfitness." Whatever the reason, a disconsolate Tom sought solace in the confessional of a Capuchin church in Manhattan. The confessor, unfortunately, was unduly harsh and told him in very strong terms that he certainly did not belong in the monastery, still less the priesthood. He told Merton that he was wasting his time and insulting the sacrament of penance by indulging in self-pity in his confessional. Merton left in tears.

He returned to St. Bonaventure's to work with the friars. He settled into life as a teacher and began to live as if he were in a religious order: he prayed regularly, taught classes, and lived simply. A few months later, looking around for a place to make an Easter retreat, Tom remembering a friend's comment about a Trappist monastery in the Kentucky hills, called Our Lady of Gethsemani.

A turning point was at hand. Merton arrived at Gethsemani late one night and was greeted by the monastery's porter, or doorkeeper. "Have you come here to stay?" asked the blunt Trappist brother. Tom was taken aback by the deeper meaning of the question.

"What's the matter?" answered the porter. "Why can't you stay? Are you married or something?"

"No," answered Merton, "I have a job."

But as soon as Merton stepped into the halls of the monastery it was clear where he had arrived. It took Merton a few months before he decided to enter the order. For him the monastery was the "center of all the vitality that is in America," and it exerted on him an "immediate and irresistible" power.

He returned to St. Bonaventure still thinking of his visit to Gethsemani and began leading a life patterned even more closely on that of a religious community. At this point, Merton had little doubt about what he had to do. Faced with the possibility of being drafted into the army, however, a decision was urgent. He finally decided that if Gethsemani would not have him he would join the army but as a pacifist. Gethsemani accepted him. He stunned his friends by resigning his position at St. Bonaventure and entering the Trappists on December 10, 1941.

The remainder of *The Seven Storey Mountain* details his life in the monastery. For the rest of his life Thomas Merton (now Father

M. Louis, OCSO) wrote numerous books on the contemplative life, on nonviolence, on Cistercian life, on Christian doctrine, and on Zen, serving as a spiritual guide for millions around the world. He filled volumes with his poetry. He maintained an extensive correspondence with writers, activists, and religious leaders of almost every stripe. He served as master of students and, later, master of novices for his abbey. He was visited at Gethsemani by peace activists, writers, poets, artists, musicians, priests, sisters, brothers, and those who simply appreciated his outlook on the modern world. He was a giant.

Later in his life he fell deeply in love with a woman—a nurse he met while recuperating in a local hospital—but chose to break off the relationship and remain a monk. Eventually he was given permission to become a hermit and live in a small house on the grounds of the monastery. He continually explored his inner life and deepened his relationship with God.

A final irony in this extraordinary life: in 1968, after years of butting heads with his religious superiors, Merton was granted permission to leave the monastery for an extended trip to Asia. On his way he stopped in a place called Polonnaruwa, in Ceylon (now Sri Lanka), where he paused before immense statues of the Buddha. He was overwhelmed by a feeling of grace, of contentment, unlike any he had ever known. "Looking at these figures," he wrote, "I was suddenly, almost forcibly, jerked clean of the habitual, half-tired vision of things, and an inner clearness, clarity, as if exploding from the robes themselves, became evident and obvious." The devout Catholic monk had enjoyed a mystical experience in front of a statue of the Buddha. A few weeks later, on December 10, 1968, in, in Bangkok for an ecumenical conference, Merton was taking a bath when he slipped in the bathroom, grabbed an electric fan, and was electrocuted. So the man who took a vow of stability in a Kentucky monastery died miles and miles away in Bangkok, called home by the One he sought in contradictions.

His was a remarkable spiritual journey. The measure of the man is found in his prayer he records is his book *Thoughts in Solitude*. It is one that anyone can pray:

> My Lord God, I have no idea where I am going. I do not see the road ahead of me. I cannot know for certain where it will end. Nor do I really know myself, and the fact that I think I am following your will does not mean that I am actually doing so. But I believe that the desire to please you does in fact please you. And I hope I have that desire in all that I am doing. I hope that I will never do anything apart from that desire. And I know that if I do this you will lead me by the right road, though I may know nothing about it. Therefore I will trust you always though I may seem to be lost and in the shadow of death. I will not fear, for you are ever with me, and you will never leave me to face my perils alone.

18

Dorothy Day

Dorothy Day is up for canonization. There are those who, with good reason, wonder how this is possible. After all, she was a pacifist, in some sense even an anarchist, arrested, and investigated by the FBI. She lived with a man out of wedlock, had a child, had an abortion. Not a promising beginning.

Dorothy was born in Brooklyn to a nominally Episcopalian family in 1897. At a young age, following the needs of her father, a newspaper man who was looking for a job, the family moved to Chicago. She eventually attended the University of Illinois, choosing a writing career and showing an interest in the pressing political issues of the day. Religion during this time was a non-issue; in fact, for her it was an impediment. Eventually Dorothy dropped out of college to make her way as a journalist in New York City. There she plunged into the bohemian world of Greenwich Village and took assignments with radical newspapers covering socialist movements. During a suffragist march in Washington, DC, she was arrested and thrown into jail alongside many other women protesters. That time in jail left a lasting impression and led her to deeply identify with the poor and abused in society. She recounts how jail prompted her to meditate on how her own sinfulness contributed to suffering and evil in the larger world.

Dorothy continued to be a familiar figure among the famous Greenwich Village writers and radicals of the late twenties and early thirties. In the early 1920s, at a party in Greenwich Village Dorothy met and fell passionately in love with a man named Forster Batterham, with whom she lived as a common-law wife in a ramshackle house on Staten Island. In 1926, Dorothy became pregnant. The pregnancy awakened something new in Dorothy: an appreciation of creation and a desire to be in relationship with God. And a second chance. Not far from her mind was a sad memory of a few years before when she had had an affair with a man she had met while working in a local hospital. She became pregnant and had the child aborted, something she always regretted and would never speak directly about except on occasion to close friends. Her current pregnancy helped her feel washed clean by God and able to start life anew. And in the soil of her gratitude grew the seed of faith. She began to read Christian classics and to pray daily. She became determined to have her child baptized, and baptized Catholic.

It so happened that living near Dorothy on Staten Island was a Sister of Mercy named Sr. Aloysia, who worked in a house for unmarried mothers and their children. The sister's simple life fascinated Dorothy. One day Sr. Aloysia asked Dorothy bluntly, "How can your daughter be brought up Catholic if you don't become one yourself?" Dorothy took her point, and so, after her daughter Tamar Teresa was baptized, Dorothy was received into the Catholic Church.

Forster, on the other hand, ever the anarchist, had absolutely no interest in organized religion, or organized anything, for that matter. "It was impossible to talk with him about religion," wrote Dorothy sadly. "A wall immediately separated us." The day of Tamar's baptism was tense. After the brief ceremony Forster left the celebration to set lobster traps for the evening meal. He returned to dinner, only to quarrel with Dorothy. A year later the two finally parted. It was a very painful experience for Dorothy, who not only feared being left alone with her child, but feared the terrible emptiness and longing for Forster. In choosing the Church, leaving him was the one incredible sacrifice she had to make. It was a stiff price to pay for her conversion, and she never got over it.

Theirs had been a passionate love: "I loved him for all he knew and pitied him for all he didn't know," she wrote. "I loved him for the odds and ends I had to fish out of his sweater pockets and for the sand shells he brought in with his fishing. I loved his lean cold body as he got into bed smelling of the sea and I loved his integrity and stubborn pride." In her early letters to him she wrote, "I miss you so much. I was very cold last night. Not because there wasn't enough covers but because I didn't have you." During a brief separation when she was away she wrote, "My desire for you is painful…I have never wanted you as much as I have ever since I left…." Letters continued for some five years after they parted forever, she pleading with him to come back and marry her and be a father to their daughter. At times she wrote in frustration, "Do I have to be condemned to a life of celibacy all my days, just because of your pig-headedness? Damn it, do I have to remind you that Tamar needs a father?" Again, trying to entice him back, "I am not restrained when I am lying in your arms, am I?" This is but a hint of the sacrifice she made in becoming a Catholic.

Her early identification with the poor never left her. During her days in Greenwich Village, she would often drop by St. Joseph's Church, where she found not only her beloved poor but also an atmosphere of prayer. And she was captivated by traditional Catholic spirituality but as she embraced Catholicism, Dorothy was troubled that the Church, though often a haven for the poor, nonetheless seemed blind to the systemic causes of poverty. Why, she wondered, did the Communists seem to be the only ones helping the poor? On a more personal level, she began to wonder whether there was a way for her to marry her concern for social justice and her new Catholicism.

An answer came in 1932, when she met Peter Maurin, a self-described French peasant who had been educated by the Christian Brothers. Peter, whom Dorothy would always call her mentor, encouraged his new friend to use her journalistic talents to found a newspaper. The paper would offer solidarity with the workers and a critique of the status quo from the perspective of the Gospels. The first issue of the *Catholic Worker* was distributed, fittingly, on May 1, 1933—May Day and later the Feast of St. Joseph the Worker. It sold for a penny (and still does). That issue sold twenty-five hundred copies. By the end of the year, circulation was up to one hundred thousand.

Along with publishing the paper, Dorothy Day and Peter Maurin opened houses of hospitality for the poor in New York

City. These centers offered food and shelter during the Depression for hundreds of men and women. Dorothy and Peter also began communal farms for the poor as another way of building community. The houses of hospitality gradually began to spread throughout the United States. For the next several decades she worked in her own house alongside other volunteers and traveled extensively, visiting Catholic Worker houses around the country. She also spent much of her time as a journalist, writing articles and editorials for the paper, while serving as a model for her followers through her presence and prayer.

Days were busy for everyone living in a Catholic Worker house. Typically early in the morning someone would rise to begin boiling water for the soup that would soon serve the many visitors at lunchtime. For a few hours the poor men and women would drop by to eat and relax, all the while talking to the volunteers. Afterward some of the volunteers, many of them young college graduates, would wash the pots and pans, while others might run to the post office, venture out for food, spend time paying bills and keeping the books, or tidy the house. In the evening came dinner, a Vespers service, and again more people to be met at the door before the house was finally locked up for the evening. Friday nights were given over to public meetings and discussions, open to whoever wished to come. At some point in the day came Mass, perhaps at a local church or celebrated by a priest in the house.

Throughout her long life, Dorothy Day adhered to a practice of voluntary poverty, living simply, wearing clothes that had been donated to Catholic Worker houses, traveling by bus, and striving to have as few possessions as possible. She would never claim tax-exempt status for the Catholic Worker. Her notion was that when you give to the poor, it should be done without getting a tax write-off in exchange. She was careful to distinguish between the dignity and freedom of such a choice and the bondage of destitution that enslaves so many of the poor. In keeping with her understanding of the gospels, Dorothy also became a tireless advocate for peace. For her, the message of the Sermon on the Mount led to an unshakable commitment to nonviolence. Her stance on nonviolence and her willingness to engage in campaigns of civil disobedience began shortly after World War II (protesting the civil defense drills of the 1950s) and continued through the Cold War and Vietnam.

As a result of this work she was shot at, imprisoned, and investigated by the FBI. This did not deter her. "The servant is not greater than his master," she would say. She received criticism even from some of her staunchest Catholic supporters who admired her work with the poor but found her pacifism a bitter pill to swallow, especially during times of war. Neither did this deter her. And in the 1960s, when public social protest became more commonplace, the witness of Dorothy Day was a potent symbol to a new generation of advocates for social justice.

In 1973, at the age of seventy-six, she was arrested and jailed for her participation in a United Farm Workers rally supporting Cesar Chavez and the rights of migrant workers. A striking black-and-white photograph taken that day shows the birdlike, gray-haired woman wearing a secondhand dress and sitting on a folding chair. Dorothy gazes up calmly at two burly, armed police officers, who tower over her. It is a portrait of a lifetime of commitment, the dignity of discipleship, and the absolute rightness of the gospel.

Among her disappointments that she never mentioned was that, despite the great comfort Day took in her daughter, Tamar Teresa, both Tamar and all her children drifted away from the Church. It was a sorrow Dorothy Day took with her to the grave. As sickness and age began to wear on her, and Dorothy could no longer maintain as active a schedule, she was increasingly confined to her room. During those difficult times she would say, "My job is prayer." She died on November 29, 1980.

At her funeral Mass held at Nativity Parish that day several odd things happened. A light fixture high in the ceiling exploded dramatically during the Mass. Then, after the Mass, as her coffin was carried out onto Second Avenue, a homeless man ran down the street, burst through the large crowd, and threw himself on the coffin, weeping. Not one bishop came to her funeral. Cardinal Cooke had asked that the funeral's time be changed, but her people at the Catholic Worker said no, because doing so would interfere with the morning bread line.

For all the measured words about Dorothy Day I'd like to end by remembering the unmeasured ones, the ones she spewed forth in the 1996 movie about her ("Entertaining Angels: The Dorothy Day Story"). It's a powerful scene in which she is praying in a church feeling the burden of opposition from outside and even from some of her own staff. Gazing at the crucifix Dorothy begins talking to aloud to Jesus, "These brothers and sisters of yours. The ones you want me to love. Let me tell you something. They smell! They have lice and tuberculosis! Am I to find you in them?—Well, you're ugly! You stink! You wet your pants! You vomit! How could anyone love you?"

But she did.

Dorothy Day stands for many things: the importance of solidarity with the poor in living out the gospel, the value of nonviolence as a way of promoting peace, the importance of community in the life of the Church. She also stands for those who think themselves too damaged or sinful to do anything meaningful for God. Her frustrating experiences with casual sexual affairs, her abortion, and her tumultuous relationship with Forster prompted her to search even more earnestly for meaning. She was a passionate woman, deeply sexual, who would write, "I could not see that love between a man and a woman was incompatible with love of God" and "It was because through a whole love, both physical and spiritual, I came to know God."

She was a person whose vocation was to work directly with the poor and alleviate their suffering, as was Mother Teresa. She was a woman whose life of prayer animated her good works, as was Thérèse of Lisieux. Most of all, she didn't let her sinfulness stand in the way of her responding to the call of God. Nor should we.

19

Pierre Toussaint

If Pierre Toussaint is ever canonized as the first black American saint, there will be dancing in the streets from Harlem to Bedford Stuyvesant. For almost seven decades this black man attended New York's oldest church, St. Peter's in downtown Manhattan. He was no Reverend Al Sharpton or Reverend Jesse Jackson but, like most saints, he quietly let his actions leave their own eloquent message as his legacy.

Born into slavery in the French colony of Haiti in 1766, Toussaint was among the 800,000 slaves who made it easy for the French plantation owners to amass huge amounts of wealth from their coffee and sugar crops. But when the French revolution exploded and the slaves lashed out with their own uprising, many of the slave owners packed up and fled. John Berard du Pithon, Toussaint's master, fled to New York City with his wife, his sister, four slaves, and Toussaint.

When du Pithon fell on hard times in the city and eventually died, Toussaint stayed on with his master's family and, for the next twenty years, supported them with the money that he earned as a hairdresser. And even beyond that, Toussaint and his wife, Juliette, who was also a slave, made their modest home a haven for orphaned black children, raised them, and eventually even found jobs for them. He also raised enough money (through his wealthy customers) for a special home for orphans that had been built by a priest and that helped those who needed food, medicine, or clothing. When, on her deathbed, his late master's wife arranged for his freedom, Toussaint dedicated the rest of his life, and much of his money, toward ransoming the freedom of other slaves. He also spent the lion's share of his time visiting and nursing those who had been struck down by yellow fever or cholera.

Pierre Toussaint died in New York City in 1853, at the age of eighty-seven. Both blacks and whites would readily agree that nothing seemed more personally important and critical to Toussaint than sharing joy by helping others, even his own slave masters.

In the eyes of the Vatican miracles play no small part in the process of canonization. And, in Toussaint's case, there is already one instance where it seems a reality. A man in Haiti had been diagnosed in 1966 as having cancer in both the abdomen and lung. He had only about three months to live. The story goes that a local priest, who had been counseling the patient at the time, suggested that he pray to a fellow Haitian, Pierre Toussaint. While the patient continued to lose weight, hope, and the will to live, the prayers to Pierre Toussaint continued. And when finally the doctors routinely examined the patient on one particular day, they found, to their amazement, that there wasn't a trace of cancer anywhere in the man's body and there wasn't a shred of medical explanation for any of it. He was pronounced completely healthy.

It seems likely that one day millions of Catholics will be venerating Pierre Toussaint as the first black American saint by way of the streets of New York. Looking at him, it was easy to catch a glimpse of God, a mirror of what we ought to be.

20

Mychal Judge

A film was distributed in September 2006, on the fifth anniversary of 9/11. Its title: *Saint of 9/11*, a touching elegy for the late Father Mychal Judge, the much-loved New York City Fire Department chaplain, who was one of the first to die at the World Trade Center when debris fell on his head as he was following firefighters into the lobby of the north tower. A famous photograph—you may remember it—shows a dead Fr. Judge, head slung to the side, being carried out by four firemen – like a modern pietà.

Let Jesuit Father John Dear tell the story as he experienced it.

> On the morning of September 11, 2001, I was having breakfast with my parents at their hotel in Manhattan when we heard that a plane had crashed into the World Trade Center Towers. My parents left town before both buildings collapsed, and I went downtown to St. Vincent's Hospital to try to help. In two days, Red Cross officials asked me to help coordinate chaplains at the main Family Assistance Center. I worked there full-time for three months with over 500 chaplains of all religion and counseled

some 1,500 relatives and 500 firefighters and rescue workers at Ground Zero. After leaving Ground Zero on Friday afternoon September 14, I stopped by the Church of St. Francis of Assisi on West Thirty-First Street, near Madison Square Garden to attend the wake of Franciscan Father Mychal Judge, the chaplain of the New York Fire Department, one of the first New Yorkers killed that terrible morning. The next day, September 15, over 3,000 people attended Father Judge's funeral, which was broadcast live around the world. He was hailed as a real hero.

Who was this man Fr. Dear speaks of? Mychal Judge was born in Brooklyn on May 11, 1933, the son of Irish immigrants. He lost his father when he was only six and missed him terribly, missed having his father to look up to. When he grew up he entered the Franciscans in 1954 and was ordained in 1961. He then served as pastor of two New Jersey parishes. In 1986, he was assigned to St. Francis of Assisi Church in Manhattan, and, in 1992, he was named chaplain to the New York City Fire Department. "I always wanted to be a priest or a fireman," he said at the time. "Now I'm both!" Within a short time, he gained the respect of every firefighter in New York City.

It was easy to see why. Mychal Judge was exceptionally outgoing, friendly, open, and extroverted. He was a great raconteur whose gift of gab was complemented by a rollicking sense of humor. He regularly talked to thousands of people—parishioners, the ill, firefighters, other Franciscans. One Franciscan recalled later that he "treated everyone like family."

About a month before he died, Mychal Judge had a strong sense from his prayer that his life would soon end, and so he decided to give away his few possessions. A friend of his received a box full of his books. Then, when word came that a plane had crashed into one of the World Trade Center towers, Mychal immediately went downtown with other firemen. Mayor Giuliani saw him rush by with several firemen and grabbed him by the arm. "Mychal, please pray for us," he said. "I always do!" Mychal responded with a nervous smile.

A few months after the catastrophe, a documentary on national television showed footage of the lobby area inside the first tower only minutes before it collapsed. Father Mychal Judge can be seen walking by slowly, looking distressed and worried, his hand and lips moving slowly. Many presume he was saying the rosary. Moments later, he went outside to bless the bodies of a firefighter and a woman. Just as he removed his helmet, steel debris fell on him, striking him in the back of the head, killing him instantly. That photograph of firefighters carrying his dead body minutes later to nearby St. Peter's Church traveled around the world. Father Mychal Judge was sixty-eight years old.

Father Dear remembers:

> During the weeks after 9/11 I met hundreds of fire fighters at Ground Zero and the Family Assistance Center. On several occasions, I came upon a circle of ten or twenty firefighters, standing together in silence, in a state of shock. I did not know what to say to them, so I would ask them about Father Mychal Judge. Immediately, their faces would light up. They always knew him. More than once, I was told about how he would enter a hall during some firefight-ers banquet and announce in a loud voice, 'You are all doing God's work, therefore, all your sins are for-given!' Father Judge had run-ins with church authori-ties. He routinely gave this general absolution. When

the cardinal of New York heard about it Mychal was called in, reprimanded, and told never to do it again. But he disobeyed and continued to offer firefighters the mercy of God's forgiveness. Many of them spoke of how grateful they were.

But it must be said that this man of many good deeds did not achieve his life of grace without struggles. He had to battle his twin demons of alcohol and homosexuality. He kept his celibacy, but it was a struggle. He did not carouse or seek sexual adventures. Because of his own struggles he worked sympathetically and closely with the gay Catholic organization Dignity. That, of course, brought him into conflict with the conservative Catholic establishment. He even marched in a St. Patrick's Day parade organized by a gay activist. In the early days of AIDS when even the medical personnel were fearful of physical contact, Fr. Judge ministered to the dying men at St. Vincent's Hospital and physically embraced them. Even when he encountered hostility from patients who wanted nothing to do with religion he discovered that rubbing their feet with holy oil before he talked with them would usually break down their resistance. That was heroic. As to his alcoholism, at the time of his death he had been sober for twenty-three years and had saved countless people by taking them to AA. One man remembers living in a box until Fr. Judge found and rescued him.

Quite a man. The bottom line came from a fire captain who said, "Father Mychal was the kindest guy in the world. He always had time for everyone." Mychal once told one of his friends that when he got up in the morning, he allowed himself two minutes for "a pity party—to feel sorry for myself." After that, he went to work, helping and serving those in need, whomever he met.

Mychal Judge gave his life in loving kindness, selfless service, and steadfast compassion. He is a witness to Gospel love, to the greatest love of all—laying down our lives in love for others. "Lord, take me where you want me to go," Mychal Judge said in a prayer he once wrote. "Let me meet who you want me to meet. Tell me what you want me to say, and keep me out of your way."

21

George Washington Carver

George Washington Carver was the great black scientist who did a lot with the lowly peanut, both medically and commercially. He made it a great industry through his scientific endeavors. Back when he lived, in the early 1900s, when prejudice was even more rampant than today, he always used to tell the black community not to let themselves be defined by those who were prejudiced against them.

Carver was a religious man, and he believed mightily in his baptism that defined him first and foremost as a child of God. And he demonstrated it the day he was brought to Washington, D.C., to the "Ways and Means Committee" in January 1921 to explain his work on the peanut. He expected such a high-level committee to handle the business at hand with him and those who had come with him with dignity and proper decorum.

He was shocked when speakers who got up ahead of him to make their presentations were treated in a very demeaning manner and harassed. Of course, as a black man, he was last on the list and so, after three days, he finally walked up the aisle to speak. On the way up he overheard one of the committee members say—and quite loudly for all to hear—"I suppose you have plenty of peanuts and watermelon to keep you happy!" He ignored the remark as an ignorant jibe, although it stung him. But worse was to come.

He was upset on seeing another committee member sitting there with his hat on and his feet on the table. When the chairman of the Ways and Means Committee told the member to take off his hat, the man said out loud, "Down where I come from we don't accept any nigger's testimony, and I don't see what he can say that has any bearing on this committee." The demeaning word stopped him in his tracks and at this point George Washington Carver was ready to turn right around and go back home. He had to struggle not to, but he pulled himself together and, as he wrote in his autobiography, "Whatever they said of me, I knew what I was, that I was a child of God, and so I said to myself inwardly, 'Almighty God, let me carry out your will.'"

He got to the podium and was told that he had twenty minutes to speak. Carver opened up his display case and began to explain his project. Well, so engaging was his presentation that those twenty minutes went all too quickly and the chairman asked for an extension so he could continue, which he did for an hour and three quarters. They voted him four more extensions, so he spoke for several hours. At the end of his talk they all stood up and gave him a long round of applause. And all because he knew who he was—God's child—and refused to be defined by the labels of his culture.

A holy man who was his own man and God's man. In short, a saint.

22

Saintly Snapshots

Here we take a break (one of three) from the "celebrity" saints to look at some snapshots of some everyday saints. Here are a dozen of them.

Madeleine L'Engle

Some readers are familiar with the writings of Madeleine L' Engle, an award-winning author and committed Christian. She has inspired many people with her work. Some of her musings about church: One Sunday, she relates, she visited a unique Episcopal church in New York. A man stood up in that church and said, "I hope this is appropriate to ask. I was an abused child. I'm terrified of being an abusive father. I need help and prayer." She knew then this was a church she could stay in. "Because people are willing to be vulnerable," she says, "this church is very different. Sometimes it gets messy, but that's okay. People are not afraid to ask questions. We're able to admit we're all broken, we've all made terrible mistakes, we're all in need, and we all want things we don't have."

She said they meet in an upper room. The building was sold, and they gave all the beautiful things to the Metropolitan Museum. "There's not a mink coat in the place," she says, "and there's not anyone else my age there either. They're all very young, very alive. The five o'clock Eucharist is largely street people—on drugs, HIV-positive, or with AIDS." One member told her it was the only place where he was called by his name. "It's a church in which a mother whose twenty-seven-year-old son has died is free to say, 'People think I'm terrible because I can't pray.' And I can reassure her, 'You don't have to pray. We're praying for you. That's what the body of Christ is about."

On marriage: Married for forty-two years to TV actor Hugh Franklin, she wrote these wise words about marriage. "Our love has been anything but perfect and anything but static. Inevitably there have been times when one of us has outrun the other, and has had to wait patiently for the other to catch up. There have been times when we have misunderstood each other, demanded too much of each other, been insensitive to the other's needs. I do not believe there is any marriage in which this does not happen. The growth of love is not a straight line, but a series of hills and valleys. I suspect that in every good marriage there are times when love seems to be over. Sometimes those desert times are simply the only way to the next oasis, which is far more lush and beautiful after the desert crossing than I could possibly have been without." These words should be repeated at every wedding.

On the Bible: "The Bible is true. It's not entirely factual, but it's true. That's hard for a lot of people to understand. Fact and truth are not the same. I love what Karl Barth said: 'I take the Bible far too seriously to take it literally.' Some of the Bible is history and some is story, and we don't always know which is which. But it doesn't matter. What I'm looking for in the Bible is truth. If you look at the great protagonists in the Old and New Testament, not one of them is qualified to do what God is asking that individual to do. (In a sense we're all unqualified.) God goes to great pains to pick the unqualified. If you were starting a nation, would you pick a woman past menopause and a man a hundred years old? That doesn't seem sensible, but that's what God did. The message is clear. If you think you're qualified, you might believe you did a good job. If you know you're unqualified, you realize you can only accomplish something because you're empowered by God." Madeleine L'Engle died in 2007.

Lisa Beamer

Lisa Beamer was on *Good Morning America* sometime back. If you remember, she's the wife of Todd Beamer who said "Let's roll!" and helped take down the hijacked plane that was heading for Washington, DC, on September 11.

She said it's the little things that she misses most about Todd, such as hearing the garage door open as he came home, and her children running to meet him. Then Lisa told about a very special teacher she had in high school many years ago whose husband died suddenly of a heart attack. About a week after his death, this teacher shared some of her insight with a classroom of students. As the late afternoon sunlight came streaming in through the class-room windows and the class was nearly over, the teacher moved a few things aside on the edge of her desk and sat down there. With a gentle look of reflection on her face, she paused and said,

"Class is over. I would like to share with all of you a thought that is unrelated to class, but which I feel is very important. Each of us is put here on earth," she continued, "to learn, share, love, appreciate, and give of ourselves. None of us knows when this fantastic experience will end. It can be taken away at any moment. Perhaps this is the Power's way of telling us that we must make the most out of every single day."

Her eyes beginning to water, she went on, "So I would like you all to make me a promise. From now on, on your way to school, or on your way home, find something beautiful to notice. It doesn't have to be something you see, it could be a scent, perhaps of freshly baked bread wafting out of someone's house, or it could be the sound of the breeze slightly rustling the leaves in the trees, or the way the morning light catches one autumn leaf as it falls gently to the ground. Please look for these things, and cherish them. For, although it may sound trite to some, these things are the 'stuff' of life. The little things we are put here on earth to enjoy. The things we often take for granted. We must make it important to notice them, for at any time it can all be taken away."

"The class was completely quiet," says Lisa Beamer. "We all picked up our books and filed out of the room silently. That afternoon," she continued, "I noticed more things on my way home from school than I had that whole semester. Every once in a while, I think of that teacher and remember what an impression she made on all of us, and I try to appreciate all of those things that sometimes we all overlook."

Michael DeBakey

Michael DeBakey was a doctor. Among many other accomplishments, he is credited with developing the Mobile Army Surgical Hospital concept for the military. You know that better as M*A*S*H—courtesy of TV and Hawkeye, Margaret, Radar, and the rest—which has led to the saving of thousands of lives during the Korean War onwards.

In addition he pioneered the development of surgical centers for treating returning military personnel, and that system subsequently became the Veterans Administration Medical Center System, saving many more lives. He was also part of the team back in the 1960s that performed the first successful coronary-artery bypass, but even before that, he invented the pump for blood transfusions that made open heart surgery possible. In addition, in the early 1950s he designed a graft for replacing diseased aortas and arteries.

That last accomplishment is especially revealing, for in making that graft, he selected what was then a new synthetic cloth called Dacron. He personally drew the design on paper, cut the fabric and sewed the prototype together using his wife's sewing machine.

It's not every heart surgeon, of course, who's a whiz on a Singer, but DeBakey learned that as a child at home. His mother was a skilled seamstress who made finely tailored clothing for her family. Eventually neighbors noticed and asked her to teach their daughters, which she did in her home. Michael was a preschooler at the time and found himself fascinated by her work, and at his request, she began to teach him how to sew as well. He became quite good at it.

But DeBakey, who died in 2008 at the age of ninety-nine, said she also taught him something else. He said that equal to his mother's exquisite needle artistry was her compassion for others. Every Sunday she and DeBakey's father loaded the family cart with extra clothing and homemade meals for the children at the local orphanage. One week DeBakey noticed that his favorite cap was among the giveaway items. When he protested, his mother reminded him that orphans had no parents to buy them caps. Then she added something DeBakey said he had never forgotten. "There's nothing that can warm your heart more that making someone else feel better."

DeBakey said his mother's words played a role in his choice of profession. He was drawn to medicine because that field allowed him to improve and prolong the lives of others. He chose surgery because it enabled him to put to use the manual dexterity he had developed as a child at his mother's sewing room. DeBakey said, "Learning to sew as a child isn't a prerequisite for becoming a good surgeon, but caring about people certainly is. I'm convinced I would not have grown up to be the physician I am today had I not received my mother's lesson and taken to heart her most poignant message—that making people feel better is the highest calling of all."

Dr. Lena Edwards

Some, perhaps, may know this name because she is someone from our own era, a physician and philanthropist. Lena Edwards was born into a strict middle-class Catholic family in Washington, D.C., in 1900. Her father was a dentist and her mother was one of the founders of the black parish in Washington, St. Augustine—a fellow African.

Lena went to Howard University and then Howard Medical School where she met and married Dr. Keith Madison. She kept her maiden name, and the couple moved to Jersey City because they were looking for an integrated parochial school for their children. Dr. Edwards specialized in obstetrics and gynecology and built up a thriving practice, including treating the poor and immigrants. They had six children, and during her nearly thirty years in Jersey City she delivered over 5,000 babies, mainly in homes. But all really was not well. She had to contend with discrimination on many levels because of her sex and her race. She had constantly to fight for medical privileges at local hospitals. She was denied residency at the local maternity hospital despite being the first national board certified black female obstetrician and gynecologist in the United States.

Her achievements included being named one of the thirteen outstanding woman doctors in 1946, a Fellow of the International College of Surgeons, and Woman Doctor of the Year from the New Jersey Chapter of the American Medical Association. Still, for all of these credentials, Dr. Lena Edwards could not escape the hatred of her times. She met the discrimination with grace and prayer. With all of these honors, this Catholic doctor and her husband choose to move to Hartford, Texas, to live in poverty among Mexican migrant farm workers, joining her son, Martin Madison, a priest of the Society of the Atonement.

In 1961, she battled the injustice of inadequate health care for poor women by using her life savings plus funds from some friends in Jersey City to establish Our Lady of Guadalupe Maternity Hospital. She finally left Texas after a heart attack but continued her medical practice in Jersey City with her doctor daughter. In 1964, President Lyndon Johnson awarded her the Presidential Medal of Freedom. She died on December 3, 1986, leaving not only a legacy of a caring doctor and of philanthropy but also a legacy of courage and spirituality: one black woman—wife, mother, physician—clinging to her faith, facing the odds of discrimination and prejudice, living the quietly heroic life of a saint.

The Woolworth Lady

The mother of a girl about eight sought relief with her child from the cold winds and snow of Philadelphia by sliding into a crowded F.W. Woolworth store. Their thin coats provided little protection from the elements, and, despite the warmth of the store, both were shivering. As they waited patiently for their turn at the lunch counter the mother held the little girl's hand and stroked her hair.

When they were finally seated the mother asked the waitress if there was any charge for hot water. She was told that the water was free. Gratefully the mother asked for a bowl of hot water and a spoon. When it arrived, she carefully measured three spoonfuls of ketchup taken from the counter into the bowl, stirred it well, added a little salt and pepper, opened a package of complimentary crackers and, eating nothing herself, watched happily as her daughter ate the "soup." Is she a saint?

Louis Saunders

There once was a man in the news who reached out to someone most of us would agree did not deserve his help. The man who reached out to help was Louis Saunders. He wasn't a rock star or a political leader or some other sort of celebrity but a Disciples of Christ minister who lived quietly and served as a pastor in Texas. So why, when he died in 1998, did a long memorial to him appear in the *New York Times*? It was because of a single act of love he performed.

Saunders was serving at a church in Fort Worth when he learned that Lee Harvey Oswald—the man who had assassinated President Kennedy and who had, in turn, been killed by Jack Ruby—was going to be buried in his town. Saunders knew that Oswald's mother was a Lutheran, so he worked the phones and arranged for two Lutheran ministers he knew to conduct the service. Everything was put in place and, when the day arrived, Saunders stopped by the cemetery to observe.

When Saunders got there, however, he discovered that the ministers had backed out; they objected to the open-air ceremony, fearing they would be exposed to snipers. The small, forlorn, and impoverished Oswald family asked Saunders to fill in, so he did. He'd left his Bible in his car, but he knew some of it by heart; so from memory he recited the twenty-third Psalm and a passage from the Gospel of John. And he said this: "Mrs. Oswald tells me that her son, Lee Harvey, was a good boy and that she loved him. And today, Lord, we commit his spirit to your divine care."

I think it is fair to say that on that date way back then in this country there was no more hated person than Lee Harvey Oswald. No one had anything good to say about him, nothing that allowed any room for grace or redemption. No one, that is, except his mother—and Rev. Saunders. And, of course, God. God cared enough to come into our world to care for the undeserving.

Bill Wilson

Bill Wilson was a Wall Street broker who woke up one morning in a hospital for drunkards. Despondently he peered up at the house physician and groaned.

"Doc, how many times have I been in this joint?"

"Fifty! You're now our half-century plant."

"I suppose liquor is going to kill me?"

"Bill," the doctor replied, "it won't be long now."

"Then," said Bill, "how about a little snifter to straighten me out?"

"Oh, I guess it would be all right," agreed the doctor. "But I'll make a bargain with you. There's a young fellow in the next room in a pretty bad way. He's here for the first time. Maybe if you showed yourself as a horrible example, you might scare him into staying sober for the rest of his life."

Instead of resentment, Bill showed a flicker of interest. "Okay," he said. "But don't forget that drink when I come back."

The boy was certain he was doomed, and Bill, who considered himself an agnostic, incredulously heard himself urging the lad to turn to some higher power. "Liquor is a power outside yourself that has overcome you." He urged. "Only another outside power can save you. If you don't want to call it God, call it truth. The name isn't important."

Whatever the effect on the boy, Bill greatly impressed himself. Back in his own room, he forgot his bargain with the doctor. He never did collect the promised drink. Thinking of someone else at long last, he had given the law of unselfishness a chance to work on him. It worked so well that he lived to become a founder of a highly effective movement in healing faith—Alcoholics Anonymous.

AA people have a verbal code when they suspect someone might be a recovering alcoholic. They ask, "Are you a friend of Bill?" or, "Remember Bill." Saints are friends. Saints remember.

Dr. Zeulke

A tiny obituary notice in the University of Portland's magazine about one of its alumni:

> Dr. Paul Edward Zeulke passed away August 8, 2007. This is the man who delivered half the people in Portland, Oregon, into this world. He set up his practice in Portland around 1950 and was on the staff of both Providence and St. Vincent hospitals. In 1981, St. Vincent honored him on the occasion of his 10,000th delivery. After he retired in 1988, Dr. Zuelke and his wife of sixty years traveled to Lesotho in Southern Africa to work in a small mission hospital where he trained midwives and did all the obstetrics and gynecology while his wife worked with student nurses.
>
> Husband, father, grandfather, physician, lifelong devoted Catholic, he worked as board president for Catholic Charities and was a founder of the Catholic Physicians Guild and Oregon Right to Life. He volunteered as a Birthright physician and the St. Vincent de Paul Food Bank.

A small notice for a big saint.

Sister Emmanuelle

Sister Emmanuelle Chinquin did not live in a regular house. She literally lived in the garbage dumps outside of Cairo, Egypt, where the poor people live. And that's where they not only live, but get their food and clothes from whatever wealthier people have thrown away. It's a dark and dangerous place. Even the police won't go there. And yet Sister Emmanuelle was there, like Advent light in the darkness. She was responsible for a clinic, a school, houses, and their precious compost factory.

Like Michael DeBakey, whom I spoke of earlier, Sister Emmanuelle died in 2008, at the age of ninety-nine. Listen to what she said about her life: "In the slum we love each other and we share with each other. In my poor slum we laugh much. And, of course, in the big modern cities the people don't even know each other. You can change people's lives if you first affirm their lives by living as they do. The word became flesh. Of course," she continued, "the ragpickers and garbage collectors are despised, and that's the reason I came here: to share their lives night and day, to prove to them that they're human beings and that they're sons and daughters of God."

Sister Emmanuelle did not consider herself a saint, but she is, in the sense that she made a radical response to the gospel of Jesus Christ. she watched him go out the highways and byways and gather in the disenfranchised, and she imitated that.

Sito

A well-known professor and psychologist named Alexander Shaia, tells the first story about his grandmother. He writes:

> I was raised in Birmingham, Alabama, in the early 1950s during the time when Birmingham was not kind to immigrants and certainly not kind to Catholic immigrants like my family, which had come to Birmingham in the 1900s from Lebanon...
>
> I was raised in Birmingham in a Semitic world-view. What I mean by that is the view that is shared by all the village people from Lebanon, Jordan, Israel, Palestine....As I grew up, I grew up the old ways with my grandparents. My maternal grandmother—Sito in

Arabic—and my paternal grandfather. I had the great honor and delight of sitting on my Sito's lap as a young child, not hearing folktales or fairy tales as children of other traditions may have heard, but for me it was to hear the gospels chanted in Arabic.

And as I sat on her lap and I heard those melodies, I learned that there was something in the gospel text, there was something underneath the words. There was a rhythm or what we might call a grace that touched my heart and held me in awe in my early years.

Now those years of hearing the gospels chanted and receiving them from my Sito, my grandmother, came together in a new way, a profound way, a true way when I was seven years old. I stood outside my Sito's house on what would have been a beautiful May evening, except on this May evening we stood with my family outside that house after it had been set on fire. Someone or someones had broken into the house shortly after sunset and they had done a particular way of burning the house which in Birmingham was the way that racists did it. They left a signature behind.

They went through the house and they gathered up everything into the house that looked like it had come from Lebanon and poured it into pile on the living room floor. And then next they went into the house and gathered up everything that looked Catholic: statues, rosaries, and put those on top of the objects from Lebanon and lastly they put on top of the pile crucifixes, doused it with kerosene, threw kerosene around the simple wooden structure, lit the match, and fled.

We horribly stood outside that burning house, made all the more horrible by the fact that we did not know where our Sito was. And that was quite unusual for her, even in those days long before cell phones, she was always on the phone to someone in the family. So we had the unmistakable impression that perhaps we were not simply watching her house burn, that we were also watching a funeral pyre. Fortunately, about an hour later she drove up. She had gone to church that night—there was a novena going on—and we joyfully received her presence but that was not the moment that most touched my heart.

It was five days later when all of my family was together yet again as we always were for Sunday dinner, and even in those days there were some seventy of us, who were gathered together, but this time we weren't in my Sito's home. We weren't sitting at a great table with fine China. We were sitting, I believe, in my aunt and uncle's basement, on metal folding chairs, around plywood tables set on wooden horses, but, as always has been true, my Sito led us in saying grace.

When she did, she sort of looked around the room—she had a way of her glasses sort of sliding down her nose—and she looked up over her glasses and looked around the room, in my memory, and looked at each one of us and held our gaze for a few seconds. Then after what was a profound silence she said simply, "No hate. No hate. No hate."

And in that moment she lifted the heart of my family into a far different discussion than the bitterness and anger that I had been hearing for five days, and she set our family on a new course. She kept our eyes on moving forward together and in love.

Jim Miller

This story may have happened, and likely it did. We're not certain but we present it here.

About two generations ago in Idaho a small boy, somewhat delicate and not too well dressed, was looking wistfully at some freshly picked green peas at Jim Miller's corner grocery store.

"Hello, Barry." Mr. Miller said. "How are you today?"

"Oh, hi, Mr. Miller. Fine, thanks. Ah, I was just admiring them peas. They sure look good."

"They are good, Barry. How's your Ma?"

"Fine, getting stronger all the time."

"Good. Anything I can help you with?"

"No, sir. Just admirin' those peas."

"Would you like take some home?" asked Mr. Miller.

"No, sir. Got nuttin' to pay 'em with."

"Well, what have you got to trade me for some of those peas?"

"All I got is my prize marble here."

"Is that right? Let's see it," said Mr. Miller.

"Here it is. She's a dandy."

"I can see that. Hmmm, only thing is, this one is blue, and I sort of go for red. Do you have a red one like this at home?"

"No, not exactly, but almost."

"Tell you what," said Mr. Miller. "Take this sack of peas home with you and next trip this way let me look at that red marble."

"Sure will. Thanks, Mr. Miller."

It turns out that for years this was an oft-repeated scenario for Jim Miller. The fact was, there were two other boys like Barry, all very poor, and Mr. Miller would always bargain with them for peas, apples, tomatoes, whatever, and when they came back with their red marbles, as they always did, Mr. Miller invariably seemed to decide somehow that he doesn't like red after all and sends them home with produce in exchange for a green or orange marble when they make their next trip. This trade off is repeated countless times.

Fast forward. The years go by. The boys grow up. Old Mr. Miller dies. The folk all come to his home where, as was the custom in the old days, Jim Miller is laid out. Among the many, many visitors are three young men, one in an army uniform, the others with nice haircuts and business suits. They take their turn among the crowd and approach Mrs. Miller, each hugging her and kissing her on the cheek. They speak briefly to her and then move on to the casket. Each young man pauses by the casket, places his own warm hand over Jim's cold one and leaves awkwardly wiping his eyes.

The evening wears on. The hour is late. After most of the people have left, Mrs. Miller goes over to the casket, looks at her beloved husband, pauses a while, and then smiles and lifts up his lifeless fingers. She already knows what she will find: three exquisitely shined red marbles.

Robert Mansfield

Remember the South African writer, Alan Paton, author of *Cry the Beloved Country*? He told a story about Robert Mansfield. Mansfield was a white man in South Africa and headmaster of a white school who took his athletic teams to play cricket and hockey against the black schools. That is, until the department of education forbade him to do it anymore. So he resigned in protest. Shortly thereafter, a man named Emmanuel Nene, a leader in the black community, came to meet him. He said, "I've come to see a man who resigns his job because he doesn't wish to obey an order that will prevent children from playing with one another."

"I resigned because I think it is time to go out and fight every thing that separates people from one another. Do I look like a knight in shining armor?" "Yes, you look like a knight in shining armor, but you are going to get wounded. Do you know that?" "I expect that may happen," Mansfield replied. "Well," Nene said, "you expect correctly. People don't like what you are doing, but I am thinking of joining with you in the battle."

"You're going to wear the shining armor, too?" Mansfield asked. "Yes, and I'm going to get wounded, too. Not only by the government, but also by my own people as well." "Aren't you worried about the wounds?" "I don't worry about the wounds. When I get up there, which is my intention, the Big Judge will say to me, 'Where are your wounds?' and if I say, 'I haven't any,' he will say, 'Was there nothing to fight for? I couldn't face that question."

Was there nothing to fight for? Or, as the gospel expresses it, is there nothing in your Christian lives worth being hated for?

Such are the saints among us.

23

Christmas Card Saints

• A HOMILY •

On September 26, the Church memorializes the feast of Cosmas and Damien. You can tell by their names that they are hardly American saints but we will use them to segue to those who are. To begin with, for us, Cosmas and Damien are hardly household names. If anything, in a culture honed by the media, Cosmas likely suggests the old Topper movies where Cosmo Topper consorts with a couple of charming ghosts, and Damien calls to mind a pint-sized poltergeist. Even way back early legend had to supply some glamour by making this dynamic duo twin brothers born in Arabia who became doctors so noble that they did not charge for their services, a practice that would be discouraged by the AMA today.

The truth is, we know nothing about the lives of the real Cosmas and Damien except that they "suffered greatly, were rejected by their elders, were killed and were raised up." That is to say: they fatally witnessed to the faith in Syria during the persecution of Diocletian: a church, later enlarged, was built on the site of their burial place: devotion to them somehow spread to the point where they rated a four-star basilica in Constantinople; and, finally, around the sixth century, their names were added to our first canon (Eucharistic prayer at Mass). Still, for all of the early centuries' attention, their fifteen minutes ran out, and they are now a footnote in Church history, a snapshot in the ecclesiastical album, a "memorial" as the liturgical note puts it.

But, sounding a theme that runs all throughout this book, I suggest that precisely therein lies their importance for us today. Fourth-century witnesses Cosmas and Damien are a memorial, that is, they help us to remember. They call to mind anonymous people in every century, including our own, who bear witness to love. They remind us of those nameless people in our own day—and they are legion—who are still being harassed, imprisoned, or killed for their faith. They bring to our attention the Church's perennial Pentecostal sub-structure, the unseen spiritual foundation that ultimately supports the Church. This is the faith celebrated quietly every day by ordinary people with dignity and perseverance, bearing a witness that often those in high churchy places fail to give. And in our desperate times today, that is no small thing.

Cosmas and Damien are indeed a "memorial," a provocative memory of the democratic presence and power of the Holy Spirit in every age. In remembering them we not only remember their spiritual kin among us today but we rekindle hope in knowing that, in spite of the nightly newscasts, they are here among us.

I don't know about you, but this kind of subterranean memory is particularly highlighted for me every Christmas. Let me say that, like you, I get the seasonal Christmas cards, a good number of which contain personal messages—progress reports, if you will. It's been a long time since I've seen some of these people—friends and mostly former parishioners—and we exchange where we are right now in life and how time has challenged or altered us. None of my correspondents are celebrities. All are ordinary people. Most, in truth, are Cosmas and Damien, hidden witnesses, hidden saints, with their taken-for-granted heroisms, dedications, and faithfulness. So, extending the theme of the last chapter, I ask you to use your imagination and picture my Christmas card friends variously standing or kneeling around a large manger scene. I will let you peek over my shoulder as I open each one's card and read his or her message.

"Dear Father," writes Steve—he's the middle-aged man kneeling by the shepherd figures, "it's been eight months now. Advent was tough to get through with all the Christmas parties, but I made it. It's hard, But, as they say, one day at a time. Steve." Steve is an alcoholic. He's fallen off the wagon several times. But he's made it eight months this time, and every day he stops in church and prays for strength. Every day he sees himself as a rag-tag lowly shepherd in need of redemption, in need of Jesus, and that puts him high on my list, way above those who think they are self made and need no one. I love Steve.

"Dear Father. We haven't seen each other for a long time and we never really talked although you were my favorite priest. And, now, after so many years, I am writing to you. I am dying of pancreatic cancer and would like to talk to you. Marion and I have never been married in church and we would like to get that straightened out. I would like to see you. David." I never knew about his marriage. They went to church. Good people. Quiet people. I see David standing with the Magi at end of their journey, the end of his journey. David is a wise man.

"Dear Father. Sorry we did not make your fiftieth. Valerie has Alzheimer's. Was diagnosed in 2002. Most days are good. Please keep her in your prayers. Ray." I was stunned to get this card. Before they moved to Indiana, Valerie and I, many years ago, worked in the diocesan Family Life Bureau. Val was one of those very bright, talented, vivacious outgoing persons. She wrote and traveled here and abroad giving talks. She was a delight to be with. It's hard to picture her in twilight living, not even recognizing her husband and children. But, I also tell you, it's easy to picture her husband, Ray, as Joseph. I can see him quietly ministering to his wife, there in the background, faithful in his devotion as he was in his marriage. The quiet man who was there to the end—Valerie died last February. A saint.

This one, after a brief message, signs himself facetiously, "Saint Jeff." Jeff is in his early thirties now, married. I remember him as a college student. He would be the one standing around the manger scene with skepticism. Why skepticism? Well, you see, Jeff went to college. There, as in every college, where diversity and political correctness rule, he was taught that there are no absolute truths. Everything is relative. One opinion is as good as another. It was considered the height of intolerance, for example, to express the thought that Shakespeare was the greatest writer of English who ever lived lest you offend someone who thought Danielle Steele was. Anyway, Jeff was there with his parents at Christmas Mass and stood with them afterward at the manger scene and was not impressed. But after college, living a real life, he found common sense, he found truth in the people around him, in the stories of heroism and devotion, in falling in love. We talked about that, and he quietly came home.

This next card in a shaky scrawl is signed simply, "Rexall." I smile. That's not his real name. His real name is Bernum Reynolds. He must be close to a hundred today. He told me his story. When he was a little boy he was taken to see his great-great-grandmother. He says, "I'll never forget the day. It was a hot, humid Sunday afternoon, and it was a long trip. I had never met her before and I wasn't real excited about going all that way to see some old woman. To make matter worse, when we finally got to her house and went inside I saw that not only was she old but she was blind and not only blind but actually kind of mean looking. And so, at first, I was afraid of her.

"'We brought Bernum along to see you,' my father said. She turned in my direction with outstretched arms and long bony fingers and said, 'Bring him over here.'

"They practically had to push me across the room, but when I got there I saw that those same hands, which I had been so frightened by, were surprisingly gentle. She carefully traced the outline of my face and ran her fingers through my hair. And then in a voice filled with love and acceptance, I heard her whisper, 'This boy is one of ours. This boy is part of our family. This one belongs to us.'

"Father," he went on, "my parents died. I was on my own. I turned my back on God but about twenty years ago I happened to stop in a church in the city and, weighted down by emptiness and sin I just sat there gazing at the figure of Christ surrounded by the saints, and suddenly those words of my childhood came back to me, only this time in the mouth of Jesus: 'This boy is one of ours. This boy is part of the family. This one belongs to us.' And I wept and I knew I was home."

Quite a story. Anyway, Bernum eventually moved into a tiny apartment above an old former Rexall Drug store—hence his facetiously adopted nickname. He is alone except for some neighbors and the "meals on wheels" folk who visit him. He recites the office daily, and every night, he tells me, since he can't sleep, he goes to the little bay window over the store, makes a wide sign of the cross and blesses the world. I tell you, "Rexall" reminds me of the Talmudic legend that says that as long as there are thirty just people in the world, God will not destroy it. He, I'm convinced, is one of the thirty. I see him standing around the manger scene like Simeon of old blessing the Child who blessed him.

Finally this one: "Dear Father, I went to see Michael yesterday as I do every day. I clean him up and comb his hair. Then I stand back and say to myself, 'My, he looks so handsome!' Father, I'm so proud of him! You should see him. Marge." What you don't know and I do is that Marge goes to see her son in the nursing home. Her son is forty-five and has been schizophrenic since his early adolescence. Marge sees him every day whether he knows her or not, and she is so proud when he "looks so handsome." She is near the manger looking at Jesus and thinking of the baby who didn't turn out quite as she had hoped, but she keeps faith.

These were and will be your Christmas cards too, won't they? This is the stuff of living. This is the stuff of being human, the stuff of dry martyrdom. These folks are the hidden presences who made our beds, put food on the table, were there when we needed them most, cried and laughed with us. They are the faithful background, behind-the-scenes saints, out of the spotlight, but in the soft shadows of our hearts, potent memorials.

I am suggesting today that we should consider that when the Church offers us a minor feast of a couple of low-level saints with unlikely names who gave their lives so fully to Jesus in the fourth century, it is also asking us to remember our own twenty-first century communion of saints, our own Cosmases and Damiens who are out there bearing quiet witness and who give us a glimpse of what God is like and what we are called to be.

NEW SAINTS

24

Mother Mary MacKillop

It was a red-letter day for Australia. On October 17, 2010, in the culmination of a cause that started in 1925, that country got its first canonized saint, Sister Mary MacKillop—also known as Saint Mary of the Cross—who founded the Sisters of Saint Joseph of the Sacred Heart, better known today as the "Josephites" and affectionately known as the "Brown Joeys" because of their habits, which in turn resembled, to the clever Australian mind, the color of a kangaroo. She is many things to different people: teacher, rescuer of poor children, founder of a religious order, national hero, whistle-blower, patron saint of abuse victims, excommunicated Catholic—there's enough narrative in her life for a dozen people.

Now that I have your attention, let's begin at the beginning.

Mary was born in Australia in 1842 of Scottish parents. Her father had once studied for the priesthood. She was the eldest of eight children, none of whom married, one brother becoming a Jesuit and a sister a nun. The fiscally inept father tried but never could make a living so that, most of the time, the children really supported the family with their small earnings. Her childhood, as she described it, was one "of sorrow." Mary started work at fourteen and later became a teacher and then a governess at her aunt's place. She taught their children as well as the other poor farm children. Here she met someone who would later influence her, the rather bizarre Father Julian Woods, the charismatic local parish priest who, by the time he died, had managed to become *persona non grata* in every diocese in Australia. Mary went on to teach children elsewhere and opened a boarding school. Teacher and priest paths were destined to cross again. Father Woods had always been deeply concerned about the lack of education for poor and immigrant children, so he invited Mary and her sisters to open up a Catholic school for poor children in a former stable.

All this experience eventually culminated in 1867, when at twenty-five, Mary became the first mother superior of the newly formed Sisters of Saint Joseph of the Sacred Heart. She and Father Woods were the founders, and it was the first religious order founded by Australians. The new order moved to a new convent in Adelaide. The order's rules were developed by Father Woods and approved by the local bishop, Bishop Sheil, who later on appointed Father Woods as director of diocesan Catholic education—a consequential move as it turned out.

The order increased. Within a year thirty women joined her. Two years later there were 127 sisters operating twenty-one schools and other charitable organizations. Their outreach expanded: schools, orphanage, homes for the aged and incurably ill. They went where the need was. They followed immigrant farmers, railroad workers, and miners into the outback and lived as they lived. This was crucial because Australia in the mid 1800s experienced a flood of immigration. Many immigrants were poor, illiterate, and unskilled. Public institutions such as hospitals, schools, and shelters were not prepared for them. The Sisters of St. Joseph were there to fill in the gap.

At this point, because it figures so much in the life of Mother Mary and the Sisters, we should point out that this new order, the Sisters of St. Joseph, was strikingly different. They lived among the people, a startling departure from convention. Further, the new order was unique in that it was independent of the local bishop.

The nuns instead were to be governed by the mother superior, and if they could not resolve an issue among themselves, they would appeal to Rome, not to the local bishop. This kind of independence was virtually unheard of. A nun was expected to submit to the authority of the local bishop. Now the local bishop, as we indicated, Bishop Lawrence Sheil, initially went along with this setup, but things soon changed. Here's what happened. As Vicar of Education, Father Woods continued to earn enemies among the local clergy, this time over his educational policies, not to mention his advocacy of the weird spiritual experiences some of the nuns were claiming to have. As a result, some of the priests tried to discredit the new order and especially Mother Mary by spreading rumors of her financial mismanagement and drinking problem. (Not true. She did take some alcohol for health problems under the direction of her doctor, a common prescription at the time. That libel, however, so persisted that it brought a halt to Mary's canonization proceedings in 1931, only to be refuted in 1951.)

But then there was more. In 1879, MacKillop and her nuns heard of allegations that an Irish priest, Father Keating, had sexually abused children. They told Father Woods, who in turn told the vicar general, who sent Keating packing back to Ireland. This did not sit well with a priest friend of Father Keating, Father Horan, who soon became the new vicar general. Playing Svengali to Bishop Sheil, Father Horan convinced the bishop that the Josephites' constitution should be changed to be brought under the control of the local bishop. So Bishop Sheil wrote to Mother Mary, telling her, "Every convent will be under the control of the local pastor. No authority to appeal to except myself. There will be no Sister Guardian, no head but myself." Sister Mary replied with the nineteenth-century version of "No way!" She wrote, "Such an arrangement would be quite opposed to the Rule. I could not in conscience remain under those changes." The bishop fired back that for her disobedience she was to be assigned to a different convent and she wrote back that she would not leave the present residence until she met personally with the bishop.

The very next day, unexpectedly, along came the bishop accompanied by four priests. He ordered the nuns to assemble. Then with all his regalia—cope, miter, crosier—he called Mother Mary forward and commanded her to kneel. Then he pronounced over her the sentence of excommunication. Naturally the nuns were shocked and wept and wailed aloud. Sister Mary, on the other hand, simply and quietly walked out, taking with her forty-seven of the forty-nine nuns. Dressed as laywomen, they found shelter with friends. MacKillop herself lived with a Jewish family and was sheltered by Jesuit priests. Though the order did not disband, most of their schools were closed. Later, to give him credit, on his deathbed Bishop Sheil lifted the excommunication. It had lasted five months.

Meanwhile, ostracized, Mother Mary MacKillop went to Rome to get approval of her order and was received kindly by Pius IX. The authorities there allowed the order to be independent but did make some changes in the area of poverty, which MacKillop accepted but Father Woods did not, feeling the ideal was compromised. As a result there was a rift between them that was only healed just before Woods' death. But he was never involved with the order again.

The order continued to expand to New South Wales and New Zealand and was relocated to Sydney in 1883 on the instruction of Bishop Reynolds of Adelaide. It received help from Jews and other non-Catholics. Still, there was still some lingering opposition from some priests and a few bishops. They still had a hard time accepting that the Josephites lived in the local community rather than in traditional convents and that a superior general administered the order rather than the bishop. At one point the bishop of Brisbane insisted that the Sisters of St. Joseph must answer to him, and Mother Mary countered by withdrawing her nuns from his diocese. Bishop Reynolds, whom we mentioned above, was also not happy. He eventually managed to have MacKillop removed as superior general, telling her he had permission from Rome to ban her—which turned out to be a lie. That wasn't the last of the skirmishes. In 1885, at the bishops of Australia's annual meeting, the bishops voted 14 to 3 to compel the Sisters of St. Joseph to submit to them. Mother Mary countered by writing to the authorities at Rome asking that they once again confirm her Rule.

Mother Mary continued her work, traveled, and founded schools. She often traveled by boat along the hazardous coastline in spite of the fact that her mother and one of her brothers had drowned in separate shipwrecks. She established prison ministries and opened "Houses of Providence" for destitute elderly women, young girls, and homeless children. In 1894, she made the 1,500 mile journey to New Zealand, where she was treated much better than in her native land. There, later, the Josephites would establish schools. Upon the death of the sister who replaced her, Mother Mary was once again elected superior. Her health continued to deteriorate, and in 1902, she became paralyzed on her right side and needed a wheelchair to get around. She died on August 8, 1909. She was buried locally but so many people came to take away the gravesite dirt that she was exhumed and transferred to a vault in a chapel in Sydney, a gift of an admiring Presbyterian.

There are several underlying motifs that we should examine in the life of this extraordinary woman.

We must recognize that her ministry was set against the background of Australia with its vast outback swatches of barely inhabitable land and dirt-poor people, a sophisticated population of urban citizens, and the tense gap between them. Australia contains a very large ethnic and religious mix, and it has as yet to achieve a national identity, a national story. Today, like most countries, it struggles with a persistent and touchy immigrant problem, and there is hostility to refugees and asylum seekers. Yet the Josephites, in the face of all this, heroically offered free education without distinction of class or race, and Mother Mary personally received friendship and support from members of the Adelaide Jewish community and other non-Catholics. No wonder St. Peter's Square on October 17, 2010, was filled with Scottish highland bands, a didgeridoo player, and the song "Waltzing Matilda," sung by a chorus of mixed voices of all nationalities and faiths. Mother Mary MacKillop knew no boundaries.

She is hailed as a feminist standing up to male power. She was not a feminist in the radical sense some would make her, but what is true enough is that she was bent on being self-determined and independent. It's been rumored that Bishop Sheil's excommunication was really payback for outing a pedophile priest but this has been determined not to be true. What was true enough is that she and her nuns courageously did speak up. She was a whistle-blower. But above all this, like Mrs. Anna in the musical *The King and I*, it was the children. Forever the children. The children and then the poor, the helpless, the homeless—all drew her attention and her labor and her love. Indeed, a worthy first canonized saint for Australia, a worthy saint for all the world.

25

Matt Talbot

This is the story of a miserable addict, an alcoholic by the name of Matt Talbot, an Irishman from the last century who was born north of Dublin in 1856 to very poor working class people during very hard times. Matt went to school off and on and at age twelve took his first job and his first drink. It wasn't long before the twelve-year-old was coming home drunk—shocking, but hardly unlike today's drunken fourteen-year-olds. His father, himself a heavy drinker, beat him, to no avail. Matt later went to work at a brickyard and proved to be a good worker. Now in his late teens with his steady pay he, like so many others, headed for one of Dublin's 2000 pubs. Alcoholism was a major problem in Ireland, and one record from 1865 showed that police arrested some 16,000 Dubliners for drunkenness, a third of them women.

No wonder alcohol was called a demon. Even though the clergy preached against intemperance, it was an uphill battle because the laborers were paid in the pubs, and so the paycheck seldom left there. Matt Talbot was in the forefront, wasting his pay on drink, money desperately needed at home. His addiction was such that sometimes he sold his boots or his shirt for a drink. To feed his habit, he once even shamelessly stole a fiddle from a blind man who earned his living playing in the streets.

No one knew then that alcoholism was an illness, a terrible craving arising from a complex disease involving heredity, emotional factors, and the makeup of the brain. Way back in 1784, Dr. Benjamin Rush of Philadelphia wrote a pamphlet suggesting that alcoholism was an illness rather than a moral failing but it took nearly two centuries, until 1958, for the American Medical Association to finally get around to that opinion. Anyway, one Saturday night Matt and his hard-drinking brothers went to the local pub. They were broke but expected their drinking buddies to treat them. They didn't. Matt was so angry that he left in a huff and trudged home and told his mother that he was so mad that he was going to take the pledge and stop drinking. His mother said, "Go in God's name, but don't take it unless you intend to keep it." Matt responded. I'll go in God's name." His mother said as he left, "God give you the strength."

And keep it he did. From that point on he never took another drink. Withdrawal, nausea, and all the horrible aftermath followed but Matt held fast. They didn't have AA or Al-anon or the Twelve Steps in those days—no friends of Bill Wilson, who founded AA in 1935, were around. Matt had to go it alone. But not quite. He had God and a devotion to Mary. Up to this point Matt had been a nominal Catholic—after all, alcohol was his god and the bar was his altar—but after his conversion he drew close to God. He started going to daily Mass. He would kneel on the steps a half hour before church opened. He made the Stations of the Cross, prayed the rosary daily, joined Catholic sodalities, and gave much of his money to the poor.

He followed ancient penitential practices like sleeping on a plank instead of a mattress and, although barely literate, did spiritual reading and found a wise spiritual director in a Monsignor Michael Hickey. He did this for years—a reformed alcoholic, a quiet saint, on the streets of Dublin. Prayer and service were his concerns.

Matt had a heart and kidney condition and, at age sixty-five, on Trinity Sunday 1925, on his way to church, Matt fell in the street and died. He was given the last rites, and taken to a hospital but because he had only a rosary and a prayer book on him no one knew who he was until his sister identified him. When his body was undressed at the hospital it was found that he was wearing chains, an old form of Irish monastic asceticism.

People at the hospital were astounded and soon word got out. Shortly after his death, people hearing of the chains, got interested in him, and stories of his holiness spread eventually right up to the Vatican. He, a sober and redeemed man, is now Venerable Matt Talbot.

For those so addicted, a saint to pray to.

26

Miguel Pro

In November 2010, a report on religious freedom revealed that seven out of ten people in the world are unable to freely live out their faith. It also found that Christianity is the most persecuted religion in the world, with at least 200 million suffering from discrimination.

It was always so. One thinks of the French Revolution that killed clergy and religious and turned the cathedral of Notre Dame into the "Temple of Reason" with prostitutes lolling on the altar. We think of the priests' holes (little secret closets) hiding priests in England. We think of the Nazis and the imprisonment and death of thousands of Polish priests. We think of the Soviet Union forcing of atheism on millions. We think today how in the very cradle of Christianity, the Middle East, Christians are being persecuted and fleeing in great numbers. And so it was in Mexico in the 1900s when the government launched a fierce persecution of the Catholic Church. This is where our story of a brave priest begins.

Miguel Pro was born in 1891 in Guadalupe, Mexico. He was a precocious, high-spirited, risk-taking child. He was quite close to his older sister, and when she entered the convent he began to feel a call to become a priest. But that would wait. There were girls to court, and the expected career of managing his father's successful business. Eventually, however, like Francis of Assisi, he gave it all up and entered the Jesuit novitiate in Mexico when he was twenty. He was there until 1914 when life in Mexico became intolerable for him: four years earlier the government had unlashed a tidal wave of persecution against the Catholic Church and it was becoming more severe. So along with other Jesuit seminarians Miguel had to flee to the United States to a Jesuit house in California, and from there, in 1915, he was sent to a seminary in Spain where he remained to continue his preparation for the priesthood. He was ordained in Belgium in 1925.

Miguel suffered from severe stomach problems and underwent several operations. Still his health did not improve and so his superiors felt that it would be better for him to return to Mexico in spite of the ongoing persecution there. He returned in the summer of 1926. Restrictions against the Catholic Church had grown even more severe. Catholics were not allowed to teach in schools. Public worship was forbidden outside of churches, religious organizations could not own property, clergy and religious were forbidden to wear their roman collars or habits in public, and priests who criticized the government were subject to five years' imprisonment. Since the churches were closed, Miguel went into hiding to secretly minister to the Mexican Catholics both spiritually and physically, especially the poor. Hunted by the secret police, like Sherlock Holmes he donned many disguises. Sometimes he was a beggar, sometimes a police officer (so he could bring Communion to death row Catholics), sometimes a businessman.

Eventually he became a wanted man when he and his brother Roberto were falsely accused of a bomb attempt against the Mexican president even though a man who was involved in the attempt testified that Miguel and Roberto had no part in it. Nevertheless the brothers were betrayed. Roberto was spared but Miguel, because he was a Catholic priest, was sentenced to death by facing a firing squad without any legal process. On November 23, 1927, at the execution site, he stretched out his arms in the form of a cross, forgave those about to execute him, refused the blindfold, and died shouting, "Long live Christ the King!" The president had the execution photographed and spread the pictures on the nation's front pages as a warning to others, although, as in the case of Edith

Cavell (see page 138), the pictures had the opposite affect of rallying the opposition. We can still view those photographs. We can see Miguel kneeling in prayer before his execution. We can see him standing against the fence with his arms outstretched. We can see a saint.

He was beatified in 1988, by Pope John Paul II, who, ironically, fifty-four years after Miguel Pro's execution, visited Mexico. I say ironically because the laws were still on the books, and the pope in all of his papal garb was technically forbidden to enter the country. He was welcomed by the president and wildly cheered by the people.

"Greater love than this…."

Post Script

As I mentioned at the beginning of this biography, the persecutions and subsequent martyrdoms of Miguel Pro and others like him are not incidents of the past. They sadly exist today. Two recent examples: In February 15, 2005 Sister Dorothy Stang from Dayton, Ohio, age seventy-three, a member of the Sisters of Notre Dame de Namur, was buried in the tiny village of Anapu, Brazil. Her ministry there was to be advocate for the poor people exploited by the powerful land barons and economic groups who were deforesting the rain forests for profit and who, over the claims of logging land, had murdered some 1,380 peasant settlers. For her efforts she was shot six times in the chest as she was on her way to meet with government officials to discuss the parceling of land for the peasants. Eyewitnesses said that she held up the Bible and told the gunmen that it was her only weapon. She was reading from the book as the bullets struck.

The second example, recorded on the front page of the *New York Times* (December 13, 2010), cites the siege of a Catholic church in Baghdad where Muslim extremists killed sixty-five worshipers and two priests. Christianity has deep roots in Iraq, long before its roots in Europe. The headline reads, "More Christians are Fleeing Iraq in New Violence." The attack is part of a campaign to get rid of all Christians, just as Iraq forced out the Jews after the State of Israel was founded. About two weeks later radical Muslims bombed another Christian Church in Alexandria, Egypt, on New Year's day killing at least twenty-one persons. This too is an ongoing attempt to drive all Christians from Muslim nations. Each day the tolls mount. Each day Christians die for being Christians.

Christianity is indeed the most persecuted religion the world, and the lives and deaths of Miguel Pro, Sister Dorothy Stang, and the parishioners in Baghdad and Alexandria and countless others bring that statistic to life and urge us not to forget the Church of Persecution.

27

Blessed Pope John XXIII

Those who remember Pope John XXIII remember him as a refreshing successor to the austere Pope Pius XII, his warmth, his larger-than-life persona, his humor. His story is best told in anecdotes.

There was his famous answer to the journalist who asked innocently, "How many people work in the Vatican?" His response: "About half of them." Once, he was in a Roman hospital called the Hospital of the Holy Spirit. Shortly after entering the building he was introduced to the sister who ran the hospital.

"Holy Father," she said, "I am the superior of the Holy Spirit."

"You're very lucky," said the pope, delighted. "I'm only the Vicar of Christ!"

When he once met a little boy named Angelo, he exclaimed, "That was my name, too!" And then, conspiratorially, "But then they made me change it!"

When he was papal ambassador to France, during a dinner party in Paris, he was asked, "Aren't you embarrassed, Monseigneur, when there are women present who wear very low-cut dresses? It's often a scandal."

"A scandal? Why no," the nuncio replied. "When there's a woman with a plunging neckline, they don't look at her. They look at the apostolic nuncio to see how he's taking it!"

Who couldn't love a pope like that? Who couldn't feel affection for a man who was so comfortable with himself that he constantly made jokes about his height (which was short), his ears (which were big), and his weight (which was considerable). But, as Jim Martin wisely writes, "To see John XXIII as a sort of papal Santa Claus is to only partly understand him. An experienced diplomat, a veteran of ecumenical dialogue, and a gifted pastor and bishop, he brought a wealth of experience to the office of pope." Yes, he was brilliant, a student of history, a savvy diplomat, an international citizen—and deeply pious. He came by it honestly.

Angelo was born in a village in northern Italy, the fourth of fourteen children. His parents were sharecroppers, who turned over half their crop to landlords and survived on what they could produce from the remaining acreage. The sharecroppers' houses all had names and the Roncalli house was called "the palazzo," the palace. But, as one biographer wrote, "there was nothing very grand about it. They shared the ground floor with their six cows." The future pope was baptized on the day of his birth, which was the usual custom. He never forgot his humble roots and said one time, amid the splendors of the Vatican, that he would like to go back and spend a single day working with his brothers in the field. He joined the seminary at age eleven and was ordained in 1904. He always dreamed of being a simple parish priest but that was not to happen. He became a chaplain in World War I, a searing experience that never left him. After the war he was appointed to various posts: head of the Propagation of the Faith, an apostolic presence in Bulgaria (an unhappy experience), apostolic delegate in Istanbul, apostolic ambassador to France, and archbishop of Venice. And then pope.

How did this roly-poly man become pope? By accident. The long-reigning Pius XII had died and the curia was looking for an elderly prelate—Roncalli was seventy-eight at the time—to be an interim figure, one who would not make waves. When the votes began to move in his direction, he calmly made notes for his acceptance speech and on his choice of a name, which astounded them all. It was John, John XXIII. The cardinals were upset at his choice of name because there had already been such a pope named John XXIII, one of the three rival popes in scandalous times of the thirteenth century when they were excommunicating one another. John XXIII eventually lost out, and his name and number were scratched from the papal lists. Choosing that name was an embarrassment. Roncalli said later that he choose the name because it was his father's name and the name of the church where he was baptized, and he also wanted to venerate two people who were so close to Jesus—John the Baptist and John the evangelist—and he wanted to restore honor to that name, for he knew that many of those who had used it in the past were hugely unworthy of the office.

Thirty members of his extended family came from their little mountain town for his coronation Mass. In a private audience they were overcome with emotion—but not the new pope, who said, "Come now, no weeping. What they have done to me is not so bad!"

He never forgot his humble origins and it influenced him to direct much of his attention to the poor. Listen to this passage from his book, *Journal of a Soul*:

> We were poor but happy with our lot and confident with the help of Providence. There was never any bread on our table, only polenta; no wine for the children and young people, and only at Christmas and Easter did we have a slice of homemade cake. Clothes and shoes for going to church had to last for years and years....And when a beggar appeared at the door of our kitchen, when the children were waiting impatiently for their bowl of minestrone, there was always room for him, and my mother would hasten to seat this stranger alongside us.

Upon his election, he was escorted into an anteroom where a Roman tailor had already two white papal cassocks—one for a thin pope and one for a fat one. But even the larger cassock did not fit the 205-pound pontiff. In the end the tailor used safety pins and covered John's ample girth with a surplice, successfully hiding the handiwork for the television cameras. And so, in contrast with his gaunt, ascetic, taciturn predecessor, Pius XII, a portly, jovial, and garrulous Pope John XXIII walked onto the balcony overlooking St. Peter's Square with a smile for the overjoyed crowds.

At the coronation Mass John XXIII declared his intent to be a pastor, a good shepherd. Shortly after he was elected pope he visited the Regina Coeli Prison outside Rome, setting off an international orgy of press reporting. There he is, a confident, cheerful old man, his soft brown eyes alight, completely at ease with himself and his audience, gesturing expressively with his big farmer's hands, and speaking with spontaneity, obviously making up his comments as he goes along. Since they couldn't come to see him, he tells the prisoners, he came to see them. He said that he comes from poor people. Then he added, "There are only three ways of losing money in Italy: farming, gambling, and women. My father chose the least interesting way." He told them that one of his brothers had been caught poaching; an uncle had done time. "These are the things that happen to poor people," he said and then added, "but we are all children of God. And I…I am your brother." The audience—from priests to politicians, from convicts to jailers—wept openly, and in the film you can see copious tears coursing down hardened faces. Then suddenly a murderer dared approach the pope to ask: "Can there be forgiveness for me?" In answer, the pope just took the murderer in his arms and hugged him, heedless of all danger to his person, let alone to his dignity. Truly a pope such as the world had never seen.

His greatest surprise, of course, was calling an ecumenical council, which would turn out to be Vatican II, the most important religious event of the twentieth century. Unfortunately, he would not live to see its end. In September 1962, he was diagnosed with stomach cancer. During his illness he told a friend, "The secret of my ministry is that crucifix you see opposite my bed. It is there so I can see it in my first waking moment and before going to sleep. It's there also, so that I can talk to it during the long evening hours. Look at it, see it as I see it. Those open arms have been the program for my pontificate. They say that Christ died for all, for all. No one is excluded from his love, his forgiveness." He died on June 3, 1963.

All during his life he kept a diary and much of his thoughts can profitably be read in the book, *Journal of a Soul*. Some samples:

"A month has already gone by since I came out from the holy Exercises [while on retreat]. Where have I got now in the way of virtue? Oh poor me!"

In preparation for consecration as bishop in 1925, he wrote, "I have not sought or desired this new ministry: the Lord has chosen me making it so clear that it is his will that it would be a grave sin for me to refuse. So it will be for him to cover up my failings and supply my insufficiencies. This comforts me and gives me tranquility and confidence."

Three years after taking over as nuncio in Paris, in 1947, he writes: "The sense of my unworthiness keeps me good company: it makes me put all my trust in God."

On the evening of his election he recorded, "O today the entire world writes and talks of nothing but me: the person and the name. O my dear parents, O mother, O my father and grandfather Angelo, O my uncle Zavario, where are you? What has brought this honor upon you? Continue to pray for me."

Shortly after that he made this entry during an annual retreat: "This vision, this feeling of belonging to the whole world, will give a new impulse to my constant and continual daily prayer: the Breviary, Holy Mass, the whole rosary and my faithful visits to Jesus in the tabernacle, all varied and ritual forms of close and trustful union with Jesus." John's relationship with Jesus enabled him to be a most charitable and kind man. He was friendly and approachable, human and funny, warm and caring, and always loving.

Perhaps the measure of the man can be seen in this story. When he was pope he received Khrushchev's daughter, Rada, and her husband, Alexis. When they came into the room the pope heard Rada Khrushchevska whisper in Russian to her husband to look closely at the pope's hands, which she described as "the beautiful hands of a Russian peasant." She could not know that her host understood her native language, and the pope was deeply moved. The pope then asked Rada to tell him the names of her children, not because he didn't already know them (he did), but "because," he said, "when a mother speaks the names of her children, something exceptional happens." He then asked her to caress her children for him, especially the one named Ivan (Russian for John). As his gift, John gave her, the atheist, a rosary, saying he knew she wouldn't wish to use it but he wanted her to have it nonetheless "because," he said, "it reminds me of peace in the home and of my mother who used to say it by the fireside when I was a child." Then he asked the couple to accept his blessing, not the blessing of a pope, which he knew they, as official atheists, they could not accept, just the blessing of an old man. They left smiling and in tears; and to this day Rada has kept the rosary and calls it "one of my most precious possessions."

Once Pope John XXIII received a letter from an eleven-year-old boy named Bruno. Bruno's letter said, "Dear Pope. I can't decide whether to become a pope or a fireman. What do you think?" And John replied, "Dear Bruno, Be a fireman. Anyone can become pope. Look at me."

We did, and we've been looking ever since.

28

John Newton

The eighteenth-century son of an English sea captain, his mother dead when he was eleven, John Newton went to sea with his father and eventually learned the sea backward and forward. When his father retired, he was pressed into service on a man-of-war but, finding the conditions intolerable, he deserted, was captured, flogged, and demoted from midshipman to a common seaman.

By his own request he was exchanged into service on a slave ship. He became the servant of a slave trader, was brutally abused, rescued by a friend of his father's and, like the permutations of a Dickens novel, he eventually became captain of his own slave ship. He became very wealthy selling his human cargo. He abused the female slaves. He boozed it up regularly. He was dissipated, wretched.

One night a violent storm blew up. The waves were the size of mountains. Newton, for all his years at sea, had never seen anything like this. The waves picked up his boat and tossed it around like a toy. Everyone was filled with panic. Scared to death, Newton did something he hadn't done since leaving his father's ship, something we all do in distress: he prayed. Shouting at the top of his voice, the slave trader said, "God, if only you will save us, I promise to be your slave forever." The ship survived.

When Newton reached land he kept his promise and, cold turkey, he quit the slave trade. He proceeded to educate himself, learned Latin, met the great Methodist reformer John Wesley, and went on to learn Greek and Hebrew. Later the old drunk studied for the ministry and was ordained as pastor of a small church in Olney, England. There he won fame as a preacher and composer of hymns.

He later became rector of St. Mary's in London where he drew large crowds and influenced many. In a nice bit of graceful irony, among those he influenced was William Wilberforce who one day would become the powerful leader in the abolition of slavery.

He died in 1807, and, if you visit St. Mary's in London you may see his epitaph-testimony on his gravestone today. It reads:

John Newton, Preacher
Once an infidel and libertine
A servant of slaves in Africa

Was, by the rich mercy
of our Lord and Savior
Jesus Christ
restored, pardoned and
appointed to preach
the Gospel which he
had long laboured to destroy.
He ministered
Near sixteen years in Olney, in Bucks
And twenty-eight years in this Church.

John Newton, of course, as we know, is the one who left us our nearest thing to a religious national anthem: "Amazing Grace," the song that praises God for Newton's conversion.

Amazing Grace! How sweet the sound,
That saved a wretch like me!
I once was lost but now am found—
Was blind but now I see.

There is an interesting postscript to add to Newton's life. William Wilberforce, who converted to Christianity, was the great English politician and anti-slave advocate. Through his tireless efforts he paved the way for the end of the slave trade in the Western world. But it almost didn't happen. After his conversion he considered leaving politics for the ministry. He wasn't sure he could live out his faith in the world of politics. Fortunately he turned to John Newton for advice. Newton convinced Wilberforce that God had called him to remain in politics and exert a Christian influence there. It was Newton who gave William Wilberforce the wake-up call that kept him championing the cause of freedom for Britain's slaves.

29

Florence and Edith

This is an account of two remarkable English nurses who lived about a hundred years apart, Florence Nightingale and Edith Cavell. Let's start with Florence. When we hear that name we tend to think of a slender young woman holding an oil lamp, with a peaches-and-cream complexion under an old fashioned bonnet, and, of course, with the face of an angel. That's the popular image of Florence Nightingale, but it probably gilds the lily. Florence must have been made of much sterner stuff and endowed with a feisty, resilient spirit, because the conditions she had to contend with would surely have broken a lesser person.

Florence really wasn't an English woman except by adoption. She was born in Florence, Italy, (hence her Christian name) in 1810, but spent most of her childhood in England. Then, at the age of seventeen, she felt God's call to nursing. That's about the age that many of today's nurses begin their training, but Florence waited until she was thirty before she received her first nursing training in Germany. A few years later she returned to London as superintendent of a hospital, but that was only for a short while. The Crimean War broke out and was inflicting terrible casualties, so, at the age of thirty-four, Florence volunteered to organize all the nursing services for the British Army.

She had no idea what she was letting herself in for. She landed in Turkey with a team of thirty-eight young nurses and took over the military hospital at Scutari. So began the daily struggle for life within the hell of human suffering. Rooms and corridors were filled with horribly injured soldiers. There was no sanitation and precious little medical treatment. If that weren't enough, Florence and her nurses had to contend with open hostility from some of the doctors who probably believed that women weren't fit for such work. But Florence and her nurses proved them wrong.

They scrubbed, they cleaned, they nursed, and they comforted. You could say they went where no man had gone before. And the quality of their caring actually began to lower the death rate in the military hospital. Finally, even Florence's most prejudiced opponents couldn't fault her efforts, and she soon became a legend in her own time. The "Lady with the Lamp," they called her, a symbol of light in a dark, despairing world.

Florence lived to the age of eighty, having written the definitive textbook on nursing training and founded the world's first school of nursing at St. Thomas Hospital of London. And that, of course, was only the beginning, for since that time, nursing has grown into both a profession and a vocation for men as well as women. Florence Nightingale—a valiant woman who made a difference.

Another English nurse would build on Florence Nightingale's legacy. Her name is Edith Cavell, once so widely known and influential and today mostly forgotten. But she was as much of a saint as Florence and we should know about her. She was born near Norwich in England. Her father was the long-time local vicar and her village was just that: an old medieval backward dwelling of blacksmiths and berry farmers. Her father was unrelenting in preaching service and self-denial to his children. It was taken for granted, for example, that before she could eat her lunch Edith had to take some of it to the poor. She may have been bored by her father's hectoring but she was influenced by it and knew in her heart early on that someday she would have to do something useful for hurt and helpless people. She chose nursing.

In spite of Florence Nightingale's efforts (along with Joseph Lister), during Edith's youth most hospitals were deplorable.

Doctors went without washing their hands, moving from an autopsy to assisting a woman in labor. Nurses were undertrained and sometimes drunk. By the time Edith went into nursing, things had improved somewhat—patients' suffering had decreased, and standards had been raised. Edith routinely worked twelve-hour shifts among patients with typhoid and diphtheria. In her copy of *The Imitation of Christ*, she had underlined the words, "He is truly learned that doeth the will of God and forsaketh his own."

While hospital standards had been raised in England, in Europe it was often otherwise, so in 1907, Edith set out to found a nursing school in Brussels in Belgium. She returned for a brief vacation in England in the summer of 1914 when news came of the assassination of Archduke Ferdinand of Sarajevo. Her family urged her to stay but she felt duty bound to return to Belgium. She said, "I am needed more than ever." When World War I did break out and the German army invaded Belgium, she found herself trapped behind enemy lines. She observed with horror the German army looting, raping, and burning, and executing anyone they thought were spies. Edith was appalled at such wanton violence and could not stomach the thought of any allied soldier being caught and shot. Although there were posters all over Brussels warning that, "Any male or female who hides an English or French soldier in his house shall be severely punished," some hospitals tended wounded allied soldiers. Doctors and nurses even helped some to escape. Though warned that the Germans were watching the hospital with increasing suspicion, this most civil and obedient of women embarked on a life of deceit and danger: she would house allied soldiers, feed them, and make disguises for them. In August of 1915, the Germans raided the house of a member of the escape organization and found letters in which Edith Cavell's name appeared.

Edith was arrested. She was made to sign a confession in German even though she did not understand German. Held incommunicado for ten weeks, she was not allowed to see her lawyer before her trial for treason. It lasted only two days. Her lawyer argued eloquently that, being a nurse, Edith had acted on humanitarian motives, but Edith was truthful and admitted that she had helped as many as 200 men to escape, and some had even written her letters of gratitude. That sealed her fate. Yet somehow Edith thought it would all work out. It did not. She was found guilty. The American legation, the Spanish minister, and others tried to overturn the sentence but none prevailed. Sadly, her own country was subsequently found to be ineffectual in preventing her death. The night before her execution, October 11, she spoke to an Anglican clergyman, "I have no fear nor shrinking. I have seen death so often that it is not strange or fearful to me…I must have no hatred or bitterness towards anyone." Her sentence was passed and then carried out the next morning at 7AM, when, tied to a post with tears in her eyes, she was shot at the Brussels firing range.

Some good came of this tragedy. Killing Edith was a serious diplomatic blunder, for within days she became a worldwide martyr and the Germans were described as "murdering monsters." She became an iconic propaganda figure. Her death caused such a storm of protest all over the world that the Germans were moved to spare the lives of thirty-three other prisoners. The news of her death led thousands of volunteers from all over the British Empire to sign up for the war and brought America closer to entering it.

Today Edith Cavell's statue, just past Nelson's, stands, unnoticed for the most part in Trafalgar Square. Beneath it are her words, "Patriotism is not enough. I must have no hatred or bitterness toward anyone."

30

Augustus Tolton

The name is not familiar to most of us, but Augustus Tolton has the distinction of being the first publicly acknowledged black priest in the United States. Here is how he got that honor.

He was born on April 1, 1854, in Missouri, one of four children. (Augustus was named after St. Augustine, the bishop of Hippo in North Africa.) Of course, being in that time and place, he was automatically born into slavery. It was ten years before Abraham Lincoln's Emancipation Proclamation. The family they served were the Elliots, who were Catholic, and they had all their slaves baptized into the faith. (There are still Elliots living in the area.) When the Civil War broke out in 1861, Augustus' father, Peter, joined the Union Army, where he lost his life from dysentery. When Augustus was seven his mother, Martha, took her children to walk to freedom by fleeing to Hannibal and then by crossing the Mississippi River. The trip was dangerous, including a ride in a rowboat where they had to duck gunshots. They got to Quincy, Illinois, which was free territory and where former slaves gave them safety and access to the Underground Railroad.

With his brother Charley, age ten, Augustine, age nine, went to work in a tobacco factory in Quincy making cigars. (Charley would die young of pneumonia). Later Augustus worked in a saddlery, and as a custodian and factory hand. Fortunately, the family was embraced by a local pastor, an American-Irish priest, Father Peter McGirr, who had come to America at fifteen during the Irish potato famine. He helped them hold on to their Catholic faith. Augustus first went to a segregated school, then to the all white St. Boniface's parochial school. The parents of the other children there were outraged. The pastor and sisters received threatening letters. A rock was hurled through the rectory window. The kids tormented Augustus, called him a bastard because he had no father. In spite of the kindness of the Sisters, he continued to encounter such deep prejudice there that he lasted only three months.

It was Father McGirr who again came to the rescue. He took all the Tolton children into his school of St. Peter's, where many of *his* parishioners protested the presence of a black students, but Fr. McKirr held fast. He preached fiery sermons on the expansiveness of Christianity to remind people what the gospel meant. The opposition eventually died down. As he grew, Augustus, an intelligent and pious lad, felt the desire to become a priest. But he was black, and the American seminaries were closed to him. His parish priests had larger (and more Christian) hearts, and they decided to tutor the young man privately.

In 1878, he was admitted to the Franciscan College in Quincy, Illinois, as a special student but his parish priests, never giving up, finally managed to have him enrolled n a seminary abroad, the international Propaganda College in Rome (where he learned fluent Italian as well as to read Latin and Greek). Augustus naturally thought he would be sent to Africa as a missionary but an enlightened cardinal at the college, knowing full well the resistance the new priest might receive, nevertheless felt that America needed a black priest. Since Americans declared themselves a democratic nation, as he heard, this would give them a chance to prove it.

So Augustus was ordained on April 24, 1886, in St. John Lateran in Rome and then returned to America. He came into New York and wanted to offer his first Mass on American soil at St. Benedict the Moor, a black parish church on Bleecker Street in New York City. The full and joyous congregation that day experienced the first publicly acknowledged black priest in the United States offering Mass in their church. The next day he celebrated Mass for

Religious Sisters in Hoboken. He was then off to Quincy, Illinois, where Father McGirr had arranged a royal welcome.

He was an associate for two years at St. Joseph's Parish in Quincy, quickly gaining a reputation as a fine preacher—even to the point of drawing many of the German and Irish Catholics to the Mass meant for blacks. He soon became "Good Father Gus" to many. His instruction classes became popular, and he labored hard to make converts but was discouraged by the poor response. He worked hard and was gracious to both blacks and whites. A local newspaper described him in glowing terms, and his church was often filled to standing room only.

It wasn't long before he was asked to speak at public gatherings. Nor was it long before racism and jealousy raised their ugly heads from both Catholic priests and even from envious black Protestant clergy. His enemies began to refer to his church as the "nigger church." Especially hurtful was the strident prejudice of the new pastor at St. Boniface in Quincy, a Father Michael Weiss, who began to refer to him as the "nigger priest." Father Weiss had come to financially rescue the parish and was jealous of the money going to the negro parish. He was losing parishioners to Father Gus. As dean of the area and through his connections he was able to force Fr. Gus to minister only to blacks, and he declared that any white donations belonged to white parishes. Fr. Weiss enlisted the support of Bishop Ryan. The bishop called in Fr. Tolton and sternly ordered him to follow the edict of ministering only to blacks. Hampered but not defeated, Father Gus continued to work hard for his impoverished parish. Then Father Weiss outright ordered Fr. Gus to go elsewhere, but Fr. Gus had been sent there by the Propagation of the Faith, and so he wrote to the cardinal in Rome:

> There is a certain German priest here who is jealous
> and contemptuous. He abuses me in many ways and

has told the bishop to send me out of this place. I will gladly leave here just to be away from this priest. I appealed to Bishop Ryan and he also advises me to go elsewhere.

Not hearing from the cardinal, he wrote again and finally received permission to go to the Archdiocese of Chicago, whose archbishop was glad to have him. Fr. Tolton transferred there in 1889, and served as pastor of St. Joseph Church. When that closed he took up his duties in a black church called St. Augustine's Association, which met in the basement of a half-finished church of St. Mary's, which eventually became Chicago's first negro parish. Father Tolton was Chicago's first black pastor. The parishioners were thrilled. This parish would become the center of black Catholic life for more than thirty years.

But the basement was no longer useful. He moved to a chapel named St. Monica's and worked toward building a much-needed new church. A woman named Anne O'Neill donated $10,000 for a new church. Fr. Tolton solicited funds from others, including Mother Katharine Drexel (now St. Katharine Drexel). In 1891, construction was started but was stopped two years later, for lack of funds. A temporary roof was put on the finished lower level, and Fr. Tolton lived in a house behind the church, with his mother serving as housekeeper. He hoped the church would be completed, but his people were very poor. Still he tirelessly ministered to them, making the rounds visiting the sick and needy and generally wearing himself out.

All along there were bright spots. Not all were so prejudiced. We have already seen the kindness of Father McGirr. The Franciscan Friars, the School Sisters of Notre Dame, the Josephite Fathers, and Katharine Drexel of Philadelphia all extended to Father Tolton welcome and support. Father Tolton was in demand

and continued to lecture at many gatherings in places as diverse as Massachusetts, New York, and Texas. In a speech to the first Black Catholic Congress in Washington, DC in 1889, he expressed this ideal:

> The Catholic Church deplores a double slavery—that of the mind and that of the body. She endeavors to free us of both. I was a poor slave boy, but the priests of the church did not disdain me. It was through the influence of one of them [Fr. McGirr] that I became what I am tonight….I was finally admitted to the College de Propaganda Fide, and found out that I wasn't the only black man there. There were students from Africa, China, Japan, and other parts of the world. The church which knows and makes no distinction in race and color had called them all…In this Church we do not have to fight for our rights because we are black. She had colored saints—St. Augustine, St. Benedict the Moor, St. Monica…She is the church of our people.

In 1897, after returning from a diocesan retreat on an extremely hot day, he had a heat stroke while walking home from the train station. He was rushed to Mercy Hospital but did not survive. Off and on he had always had some bouts of illness. He died that night at the age of forty-three. His body was brought back to Quincy, where he was buried in St. Peter's cemetery. He had a large funeral, according to the newspapers, "four blocks long plus streetcars…" Even in death he apparently faced prejudice even though it was remarkable that, back in 1897, he was allowed burial in a white cemetery at all. He was placed deep in the ground so that a white priest could be buried above him, and his inscription is on the backside of the large cross that marks the other priest's grave.

It was only fitting that more than a century later, in the 2009–2010 Year for Priests, while Chicago was looking for some Chicago priest to serve as a model, many thought of Fr. Tolton. The Cardinal of Chicago lost no time in setting in motion the process of canonization. In Missouri a regional high school was built in his honor.

The slave boy had come a long way. So, by this time, had the Church.

31

Victoria Rasomanarivo

In 1848, a girl was born in Madagascar. She was a princess of the ruling family. Her name was Victoria and she, like Father Augustus Tolton, was black. She was well educated and raised to follow the native ancestral religion of her parents. She attended the school for girls run by the Sisters of St. Joseph, who evidently made such a deep impression on her that she took instructions in the Catholic faith. At fifteen Victoria shocked her parents by announcing that she wanted to become a Catholic. She even wanted to become a nun, but the sisters felt she could do more good outside the convent by being a witnessing Christian. The sisters also knew also that her becoming a nun would anger her guardian, her powerful uncle. Besides, at the time, the Catholic religion, like other Christian traditions, was often persecuted on that island, for even though Christianity was brought there in the sixteen century, the ancestral religion pretty much held sway. In fact, a year after Victoria's birth the queen ordered a severe persecution of Christians. Two thousand were captured and imprisoned. Some were burned alive and others thrown off a cliff. The queen's son reversed the policy when he came to the throne, but he was assassinated after two years, and the persecutions resumed. So Victoria knew what she was getting into.

Her parents were, of course, upset at Victoria's decision, and her guardian, her uncle, tried to talk her out of it. They forbade it, threatened to cut her off from the family and, most ominously, threatened her with the warning that she would have to forfeit the right to be buried in the family tomb. In that society this was the ultimate punishment, the ultimate shame. Still, nothing could be done to deter Victoria, and she did become a Catholic. Her family, against her will, then arranged a marriage with the prime minister's son, thinking he would change her mind. She was even allowed to have a Catholic priest witness it. The marriage didn't work out. She remained a dutiful wife although, like Catherine of Genoa, it must have been a challenge for her because her husband was a drunken womanizer who thought nothing of boldly bringing other women home with him. Her family advised her to divorce him but she felt that, as a princess, she did not want to give a bad example, So she put up with this embarrassment for twenty-three years, until his death. But her final influence prevailed: her husband, the object of her prayers, was baptized on his deathbed.

Now a widow, Victoria devoted herself even more to prayer and helping the poor, the imprisoned, and the lepers. She remained steadfast and even cheerful in her faith even when in 1883, the government decided to throw out all the Catholic priests and locked the doors of all the churches. Everyone submitted and cowered— except Victoria. This black woman, this princess, stood up to the government officials, insisting again and again that the churches remain open, and she said right to their faces, "You can put me to death but you have no right to shut the church." Because of her persistence (and status) the churches eventually reopened. There were still no priests but—and here she is a very modern woman— Victoria refused to be deterred.

Victoria herself led the Catholic Church in Madagascar. She saw to it that religious instructions and Sunday prayers took place. In times of persecution, many Christians found refuge and help with this woman. When the Jesuit priests finally returned to the island, they were amazed with the organization, strength, and spirit they found in the local churches—all thanks to a determined black church leader named Victoria.

She is now Blessed Victoria Rasomanarivo, the first person in Madagascar to be beatified. She died in 1894, after a brief illness. One ironic note: against her wishes, she was buried in the family tomb after all. The family, who at one time excluded her, now seemed eager to have her.

And we should be eager to have her or at least know about this woman, this lay leader of the Church, one we would call today a lay ecclesial minister.

32

Jean Vanier

It was her first Christmas there, and Kathleen Berken will never forget it. She writes:

> After my shower, I walked back through the kitchen and core member Gertie stopped me and pointed to the kitchen table…I looked over…and noticed that she had set a place for me with my favorite plate, a

small bowl, a container of cottage cheese, two pieces of toast, my favorite mug filled with water, and a little jelly glass filled with orange juice. She pointed to the table with both hands as if to make a presentation and smiled, "I did this all for you." A woman with no teeth and a huge heart and more hugs than any person clinically needs in a day graced with the best Christmas present in the world. (*Walking on a Rolling Deck: Life on the Ark*)

She was talking about the hospitality house called L'Arche, a series of homes for adults whom we formerly called retarded but whom, in a more sensitive world, we call developmentally challenged or developmentally disabled. Whatever the label, these are people with all of the emotional needs and bodily demands of infants and children, but so often without their disarming charm. Some in ages past killed them, imprisoned them, hid them, and segregated them. They were always at best an embarrassment. And then there were those who loved them and took them in. One such is Jean Vanier.

In 1964, Jean Vanier was looking for this true vocation. He had tried several as he could afford to do. He was, after all, the son of a diplomat and future Governor General of Canada. He was born in Geneva, Switzerland, in 1928, one of five children, while his father was in diplomatic service there. At the early age of thirteen he was admitted to the Royal Naval College in England, served as an officer, and resigned his commission in 1950. He was restless. Something more beckoned, and he didn't know what it was. He traveled looking for his purpose in life. He was a spiritual pilgrim. The seeding of his calling was begun on one of his trips to France. He had gone to join up with a Dominican priest named Fr. Thomas Philippe who was the head of a small community of lay students who gathered for prayer and study to help them become more committed Christians. Vanier eventually took over the group when the priest became ill, and he stayed as director for six years. Jean then returned to school to get his doctorate and begin a teaching career.

But shortly after this, he went to visit his old mentor, Fr. Philippe, who had become a chaplain for mentally handicapped men. The priest spoke movingly to him about the plight of the mentally and physically handicapped adults living minimal and miserable lives in institutions. Vanier thought long and deeply about this, and soon after he bought a small dilapidated house which he called Noah's Ark or simply L'Arche. In August 1954 he brought in two handicapped men to live with him, and from that small seed the L'Arche movement would grow into over 137 communities worldwide. Erie, Pennsylvania, was the site of the first American community, founded in 1972.

Vanier's vision was a gospel one—that L'Arche would be a place of safety and belonging. Normal and able-bodied people would live together with the physically and mentally disabled in a community of mutual help, love, and respect. All of this was based on the truth that each person is unique and each person is to be nurtured. L'Arche was to be a community of service and love. And it is. As some say, L'Arche is a place where God dwells. Later Jean founded Faith and Light, a movement of annual retreats where people with developmental disabilities and their families and friends could meet to talk, exchange about their hardships and difficulties, and pray together. In 1972, he led a pilgrimage of 12,000 disabled people to Lourdes. Vanier has since stepped down from the leadership of L'Arche to spend more time with the people in this global network. He has given his life to those who have been marginalized, those, as he says, we lock away and think worthless. He is, as one newspaper says, "a Canadian who inspires the world." He has written a number of best-selling books about building community based on love.

One celebrated figure, the spiritual writer Henri Nouwen, accepted Jane Vanier's invitation to make L'Arche his home. There he met Adam, who changed his life. Adam was misshapen, unable to walk, talk, feed, or dress himself, yet he challenged Nouwen and touched his heart profoundly. As Nouwen bathed, dressed, and fed Adam each day he became more defenseless himself, more open to Adam's brokenness as a window to God. When Adam died, Nouwen wrote of him movingly in his last book, aptly titled, *God's Beloved*.

Some of Vanier's spiritual wisdom:

> "To be lonely is to feel unwanted and unloved, and therefore unlovable. Loneliness is a taste of death. No wonder people who are desperately lonely lose themselves in mental illness or violence to forget the inner pain."

> "When people love each other they are content with very little. When we have light and joy in our hearts, we don't need material wealth. The most loving communities are often the poorest. If our own life is luxurious and wasteful, we can't approach poor people. If we love people, we want to identify with them and share with them."

> "Growth begins when we start to accept our own weakness."

This is man of great compassion, gentleness, and a reverence for life, a saint for our time.

33

Mother Teresa

In the gospels the apostles said to the Lord, "Increase our faith." There is probably no one who has not heard that these words, or something like them—and they are words that must have been constantly on the lips of Mother Teresa of Calcutta. Yes, the world was stunned to hear that a new book, a collection of her personal letters titled *Mother Teresa: Come Be My Light* is not a book of pious meditations as the title might suggest, but a book of one woman's agonizing doubt and terrifying inner darkness. "In my soul I feel that terrible pain of loss—of God not wanting me—of God not being God—of God not existing." Mother Teresa wrote those tremulous words to her confessor in 1959. Moreover, they are words describing how she felt for nearly fifty years. Yes, unknown to us, for nearly fifty years Mother Teresa suffered doubt, despair, and dryness of soul—that spiritual dark night as it is called. "In my heart," she wrote, "there is no faith—no love—no trust—there is so much pain—the pain of longing, of not being wanted—[yet] I want God with all the powers of my soul."

This draining, horrifying spiritual frustration, this feeling of God's absence is common enough especially when people are hit by tragedy. You know: "where was God when my child died?" Other saints have also felt the dark night of the soul. One thinks of St. John of the Cross, St. Paul of the Cross, founder of the Passionists, St. Ignatius of Loyola, founder of the Jesuits, and St. Thérèse of Lisieux who once confided to the sisters in her convent, "If you only knew what darkness I am plunged into!"

The thing is, it wasn't always that way for Mother Teresa. She was born Agnes, a devout Catholic girl from Albania with good parents. Inspired by a parish mission at eighteen, she joined the Sisters of Loreto in Ireland and soon was sent on a mission to India to work in a girls' school in Calcutta. In 1937, she professed her vows in that order. But nearly ten years later, in 1946, she underwent some intense mystical experiences that included hearing the voice of Jesus, who asked her to begin working with the poorest of the poor. Thus called, she soon left the Sisters of Loreto to found a new order. During that time she made a private vow "to drink only from Jesus' chalice of pain."

Little did she know that her vow would be fulfilled so literally. As those dazzling initial mystical experiences faded, the dark night of doubt and a harrowing sense of God's absence settled deep into her soul. At one point her spiritual counselor suggested that perhaps God was inviting her to identify with the abandoned Christ on the cross, and this thought sustained her. Nevertheless, the darkness persisted. It agonized her to live with it every day, year after year, even while she was going around famously doing heroic deeds. She felt deeply the burden of everyone calling her a living saint while all the time she carried this frightful doubt, this darkness, this depression in her heart. She felt at times like a hypocrite.

What a poignant story hers is! It's hard to imagine living like that for so long, nearly half a century! We ask, why would God allow this? We can only guess at some hindsight suggestions. Mother Teresa, like many leaders was a forceful personality and impatient to have her order approved. She was loaded with honors and fame and even won the coveted Nobel Peace Prize. Did her spiritual trials temper what might have been a pride that would have compromised her mission? We don't know. What we do know is that maybe her letters, which she had hoped would be destroyed, might, now that she is dead, take on a new life and move her mission and influence in another direction. Maybe, instead of helping the poor she may now have a new calling. As Blessed Teresa of Calcutta she may become the patron saint of the spiritually depressed, the doubt-filled, the skeptical.

She is, I am suggesting, a new kind of hero. She was no well-meaning do-gooder as some would have characterized her. No, remember, faced with intense inner turmoil she nevertheless faithfully responded with works of charity. In other words, put side by side her unrelieved spiritual dryness together with her stunning earthly accomplishments and you have an extraordinary woman, a saint. More than that: you have someone to inspire and coax the depressed, the doubtful, the unbeliever, to move beyond their own inner turmoil to works of mercy. After all, it's hard to think of anyone else who accomplished so much with so little spiritual sustenance. "My soul is like a block of ice," she once wrote—but not her actions, which were full of the warmth and fire of compassion. She may well be the saint of those burdened with inner dryness but who are called upon to scatter love and charity anyway.

Some feel little or no spiritual consolation. Some yearn to know Christ but come up blank. Some envy those who seem to have a sweet and easy intimacy with God, whose prayer life soars, whose faith is confident, whose joy is palatable—but none of this is for them. Faced with this, the temptation is to withdraw, to brand oneself as a hypocrite, to dismiss God, who seems to have dismissed them. But Mother Teresa shows us another way. That may be her ultimate gift. She teaches us that, rather than withdraw into the darkness, work from it. Love and serve your neighbor even when you would rather collapse into yourself. Minister to those who need you even when your needs are greater. Go to church where the community gathers, even though you'd rather be alone. Pray the prayers even out of rote. Sing the songs even if there is no joy. Receive the Lord in the Eucharist even when you're not sure he's present. In other words, to give out of one's spiritual nothingness as did Mother Teresa is the highest form of love, for it assumes a surrender to a God who may or may not be there. It's a gamble of faith that only saints can make.

Finally those painful letters of Mother Teresa at least let us know that not all saints bask in privilege and spiritual joy with special access to God that makes their work easier. No, Mother Teresa tells us that holiness is a goal for all even those who experience no joy and are buffeted by doubt and darkness. She spells out forcefully that fidelity does not depend on feelings or emotions. She was faithful to her call from God even when God seemed to have withdrawn from her, and she inspires us to do the same.

So she might, after all, turn out to be a saint uniquely for our times. Anyway, wherever we are on the spiritual journey, her desire is our desire: "Lord, increase our faith."

With that being pondered, let us close with one of the many humorous stories that Mother Teresa provoked.

God greets Mother Teresa at the Pearly Gates. "Thou art hungry, Mother Teresa?"

"I could eat," she replies.

God then opens up a can of tuna and reaches for a chunk of rye bread and they share it.

While eating this humble meal, Mother Teresa happens to look down to hell and sees the inhabitants devouring huge steaks, lobsters, pheasants, pastries, and wines. Curious, but deeply trusting, she remains quiet.

The next day God again invites Mother Teresa to join him for a meal. Again, it's tuna and rye bread. Again, Mother Teresa can see the denizens of hell enjoying caviar, lamb, truffles, and chocolates. Still Mother Teresa says nothing.

The following day mealtime arrives and another can of tuna is opened. Mother Teresa can contain herself no longer. Meekly she says, "God I am grateful to be in heaven with you as a reward for the obedient life I led. But here in heaven all I get is tuna and a piece of rye bread and in the Other Place they eat like emperors and kings! Forgive me, Lord, but I just don't understand…"

God sighs, "Let's be honest, Mother Teresa," he says, "For just two people, does it pay to cook?"

34

St. Damien of Molokai

Some thought he was heroic, others just plain crazy.

Let's go back to the beginning. Joseph de Veuster, one of seven children, was born in Belgium in 1840. He had to leave school at thirteen to work on the family farm. At nineteen he joined the religious community of his brother Auguste, the Congregation of the Sacred Hearts of Jesus and Mary, taking as his religious name Damien after the fourth-century martyr Damien, a martyr who is always paired with another martyr, Cosmas, in the Church's calendar (September 26). His superiors did not think much of his intellectual abilities and considered him not quite the right material for the priesthood. Regardless, Damien continued to pray to the patron of missions, St. Francis Xavier, to be sent abroad, for this was an era of very active Christian missionary work, both Catholic and Protestant, throughout the Pacific. He wanted to be part of it. His chance came when his brother, who had been assigned to work in the Hawaiian Islands, fell sick and was unable to go. Damien took his brother's place. After arriving in Hawaii in May of 1864 he was permitted to be ordained in Honolulu. He was greeted, not unexpectedly, by the staunch anti-Catholicism of the times. He was assigned to the mission at North Kohala on the island of Hawaii.

Meanwhile, the many traders and sailors to the islands had imported new diseases, including syphilis and leprosy, the latter being especially considered both highly contagious and incurable. At that time very few had any knowledge of the ravaging disease of leprosy (Hansen's disease). More often than not, leprosy was looked upon as a curse from an angry God, not a medical condition. That was easy to understand. The disease was relentless, full of the stench of rotting disfiguring flesh. The alarmed government soon set up quarantined leprosy settlements on the remote peninsula of Molokai. It provided supplies and food but very little medical care. Eventually the people there, isolated and sick, fell into social anarchy.

Nine years later Damien volunteered for a routine three-month assignment to the dreaded Molokai. Three months was the limit that any compassionate bishop felt he could require of anyone, given the high risk involved. Damien soon got to work with his small congregation as he built a parish church, attended to the lepers, dressed ulcers, built coffins (more than 600 of them), and dug graves. Echoing St. Paul, he wrote to his brother, "…I make myself a leper with the lepers to gain all to Jesus Christ."

Forcing himself to endure the wretched sights, smells, and horrors of leprosy without flinching, Damien decided to stay on permanently to care for the people's spiritual and physical needs. As time went on he lobbied the government for more support. He eventually saw that there were new houses and a church, school, and orphanage. He was successful in getting some Franciscan Sisters to come and work there. In time he drew associates who were willing to work with him from all parts of the globe and from all walks of life, some of whom, like the Union Army veteran Joseph Dutton, became heroic in their own right. Under him things were generally transformed. Laws were reinforced, shacks painted, and working farms organized.

Damien himself eventually contracted leprosy. The story is that every Sunday he would begin his sermon with the phrase, "You lepers." One day, after his missionary rounds, he came home, foot sore and weary and sought comfort in soaking his feet in a tub of water. When he put his foot into the hot water, he could feel nothing. Instantly he knew he had contracted leprosy. The following Sunday he began his sermon with "We lepers…" The news spread like wildfire. Damien's prayer was answered: he had made himself a leper for the sake of lepers. This did not stop Damien as he worked harder than ever to build homes and provide programs that he hoped would last after he was gone.

Damien received treatment from a Japanese doctor, Dr. Manannao Goto, who became one of his best friends. The doctor was successful in helping relieve the symptoms of leprosy but could not stop it. News of Damien's disease and work spread. At last, arm in sling, his foot in bandages, his leg dragging, he knew the end was near. He became bedridden, made his confession and renewed his vows on March 30, 1889, received the last rites on April 2, and died on April 15, 1889 at forty-nine.

As he wished, he was buried in Kalaupapa, but in 1936, the Belgium government, knowing by that time that they had a celebrity on their hands, had the body transferred to the university city of Leuven. But after his beatification the remains of his right hand were returned to his original grave in Hawaii.

At one time the king of Hawaii bestowed an honor on Damien and the Island's princess presented him a medal (which he never wore). Later, after Damien's death, she shared his story with the world. As a result Damien's name spread across the United States and Europe, and Protestants and Catholics began to send money and supplies. Damien had caught the attention of the media of the time.

But not all were happy with this posthumous fame and adulation. Anti-Catholic bias persisted. One notorious example is a minister of the Presbyterian church in Hawaii, a Rev. C.M. Hyde. In a letter to a friend that was widely circulated, he referred to Damien as "a coarse, dirty man" whose leprosy should be attributed to his "carelessness." Now it so happened that that same year (1889) Scottish author Robert Louis Stevenson (a Presbyterian) arrived with his family for an extended stay in Hawaii. While there he stayed a week at Molokai during which he kept a diary. Impressed by what he saw, he afterwards wrote a famous letter in defense of Damien answering Hyde point by point. Damien's champions would continue. Mahatma Gandhi defended him citing him as an inspiration for his social campaigns in India. He was held in high regard by President Theodore Roosevelt and Mother Teresa. He had his defenders among the Anglicans.

Damien was not without his faults. He could be quite short-tempered and seem to have suffered from some depression or "dark nights of the soul." The Church reviewed his faults and the criticisms of him but in the end found that, on balance, this man was a saint, and on June 4, 1995 Pope John Paul II beatified him. In October 11, 2009 Pope Benedict XVI canonized him. Damien's feast day is April 15, the same day that the Anglican Church honors him in their liturgical calendar.

In our day, Damien, by extension, has become the apostle of the exiled and a model of how society should minister to HIV/AIDS patients. He is ecumenically popular with several denominations whose ministries bear his name.

A courageous man of deep faith and deeper love.

35

Private Schultz and
Sergeant Ponich

This account is a brief one about a German soldier named Schultz. At the mention of that name, readers of a certain age will immediately think of the TV series, "Hogan's Heroes" one of whose main characters was a sergeant of that name, Sergeant Schultz, the rotund, easily duped clown whose favorite bewildered exclamation was, "I know nothing!" World War II and being German is the only association between these two soldiers.

Private Schultz is but a blip in a large, horrendous war that killed millions. His was a small voice and a hidden witness that came to light only later. Yet he is one of our underground saints. This is his story. Private Joseph Schultz was sent to Yugoslavia shortly after the invasion of that country. He was a loyal, young German soldier. One day the sergeant called out eight names, his among them. They thought they were going on a routine patrol. They hitched up their rifles and set out on their journey. Soon they were approaching a hill, still not knowing what their mission was. Before long they could see that standing on the brow of that hill there were eight Yugoslavias, five men and three women. It was only when they got about fifty feet away from them, when any marksman could shoot out an eye of a pheasant, that the soldiers realized what their mission was.

The eight soldiers were promptly lined up. The sergeant looked around, barked out, "Ready!" and they lifted up their rifles. "Aim," and they got their sights. And then suddenly, in the momentary silence that prevailed, there was heard the thud of a rifle butt against the ground. The sergeant, and the seven other soldiers, and those eight Yugoslavians stopped and looked. As they looked in astonishment, Private Joseph Schultz dropped his rifle and started walking toward the Yugoslavians. His sergeant called after him and ordered him to come back, but he pretended not to hear him.

Instead he walked the fifty feet to the mound of the hill, and he joined hands with the eighty Yugoslavians. There was a moment of silence, the sergeant hesitated and then he yelled, "Fire!" And so Private Joseph Schultz died, mingling his blood with those innocent men and women. Later, someone found a piece of paper sewn into his coat. It was an excerpt from St. Paul: "Love does not delight in evil, but rejoices in the truth. It always protects, always trusts, always hopes, and always perseveres."

Private Schultz is one of the many saints that lived in a time of unbelievable horror, a pinpoint of light in the darkness. Like the men in the following story.

In April of 1986 two gray-haired men greeted each other warmly in Tokyo's International Airport, Both had tears in their eyes. One man was an American named Ponich and the other was a Japanese named Ishibashi.

The last time these two men met was forty years before in a cave in Okinawa. At that time, the American, Sergeant Ponich, was holding a five-year-old Japanese boy in his arms; the boy had been shot through both legs. Ishibashi happened to be hiding in a dark corner of the same cave.

Suddenly Ishibashi leaped from his hiding place and aimed his rifle at Ponich and prepared to fire point black. There wasn't a thing Ponich could do. He simply put the five-year-old on the ground and took out his canteen and began to wash the child's wounds. If he had to die, he thought, what better way to die than performing an act of mercy. Ishibashi watched in amazement. Then, slowly, he lowered his rifle. Minutes later Ponich did something that Ishibashi never forgot. He took the child in his arms, stood up, bowed in gratitude to Ishibashi, and took the child to an American field hospital.

How did the two happen to meet again after all those years? In 1985, Ponich wrote a letter to a Tokyo newspaper thanking the Japanese people for the soldier who had spared his life forty years before in that cave in Okinawa. Ishibashi saw the letter and contacted the newspaper, who set up the meeting. The meeting between these two saints was long and affectionate.

"Blessed are the merciful, for they shall receive mercy" (Mt 5:7)

36

Paul Rusesabagina and the Benebikira Sisters

The name Rwanda calls up the horrible memory of genocide when radical Hutu-led Interahamwe slaughtered some 800,000 Tutsi. This unimaginable horror started on April 6, 1994. Shamelessly, it must be reported, no foreign aid came either from the United Nations or its powerful western countries until it was all over.

The people were on their own. Some, like Paul Rusesabagina, stayed. His story is told in the award-winning movie *Hotel Rwanda*. He was manager of a local hotel, and when the Hutu militants began a brutal assault against their Tutsi neighbors, Paul, himself of mixed background—his father was a Hutu and his mother a Tutsi—risked his life by turning his hotel into an impromptu refugee camp for the 1,200 desperate people who sought refuge there. Paul had connections with high-placed military leaders and business leaders. He knew how to bribe soldiers. He called in every favor he was owed. He was determined to save as many as he could while trying to protect his own life.

When the violence broke out he brought his Tutsi wife and three children to the hotel, but when the Hutu threatened to enter it he hustled his wife and children into a getaway truck while he stayed behind to help the refugees. Unfortunately the truck was caught and forced to return to the hotel. Everyone had been beaten, especially his Tutsi wife, who ultimately wound up losing her mother and four nieces and nephews. Finally, at the end of a hundred days of slaughter, the Tutsi pushed the Hutu into the Congo. After the massacre Paul took in orphans and took them with him into Tanzania. Then, after receiving threats to his life, he moved to Brussels in 1996.

Let it be noted that Paul credits two heroes with giving him the courage he needed in that critical hour: his father and Nelson Mandela. His father had been well respected in the community. He was a wise man, and he always told the truth. When there were disputes in the community, the elders called on Paul's father to mediate. He was so honest that if one party in a dispute was lying, they often confessed their lie as soon as they saw Paul's father. His noble character made him influential in his community. Nelson Mandela, former president of South Africa, inspired Paul because he used nonviolence and communication to bring about peace between enemies. Paul claims that the examples of his father and Nelson Mandela inspired him as he faced murderous mobs during the Hutu massacre.

After the genocide we can only imagine the emotional and physical devastation that was left behind—and the bitterness between the two peoples. But there was some ray of hope. There were other heroes. When the genocide ended a religious order of nuns called the Benebikiras ("Daughters of Mary") was there to help. Half of

Rwanda being Catholic, this order was founded in 1919 to educate children and especially women, a cultural novelty. After the genocide the Sisters found themselves caring for some 350 traumatized orphans, many of whom had witnessed the murders of their parents. The nuns stayed on during the genocide when so many religious leaders let their people down. It was a risky thing to do since they refused to segregate themselves into ethnic groups or to not give shelter to refugees. Before and during the hundred days of horror, these nuns remained faithful to the poor. To this day they bring together the families of both Hutu and Tutsi, asking no questions about the past, offering hope for the future proclaiming, "We want to build our country, our relationships, a new life. We are no longer seen as Tutsi or Hutu. We live together. We are no longer separate. We are Rwandans."

37

Brother André

Like Brother Solanus (Barney) Casey of chapter 15, Alfred Bessette, better known as Brother André of Montreal, was a doorkeeper. Like Barney Casey he had a rough start in life. He was born in 1845 in a small village some fifty miles southeast of Montreal and was so frail that he was given an emergency baptism. If Barney Casey was one of sixteen children, André was one of twelve, two of whom died in infancy. Times were hard and his father moved to Quebec to seek work as a lumberman where, tragically, he lost his life in an accident. His mother, left with ten children, had no choice but to put them up for adoption. She kept frail André and went and lived with her sister. She would die of tuberculosis three years later. Not the most auspicious beginning.

His aunt and uncle tried to get André work here and there but his chronic poor health made any kind of labor difficult, as he went from being a tinsmith, to blacksmith, to baker, to shoemaker, to wagon driver. The result is that he wound up illiterate with no trade. In 1863, at age eighteen, he made an attempt at working in the United States (Connecticut). He later returned to Canada, where the pastor of the local church noticed the young man's piety. He eventually decided to present André as a candidate to the newly formed order of the Congregation of the Holy Cross. We need to recall that this was in the time after the anti-clerical French Revolution that had suppressed religious orders in France, and teachers were sorely needed. The Congregation of the Holy Cross was formed to fill this need. They migrated to Montreal in 1847 to continue their mission. André was impressed by these valiant men, but in truth they were not impressed by him. His frail health and illiteracy were liabilities they were not ready to take on. It was finally only through the intercession of the local archbishop that they did so. André was allowed to take temporary vows (they were still nervous about his poor health and there was talk about dismissing him), given the name Brother André, and taught to read. He made his final profession on August 22, 1872.

André was immediately assigned where he could do no harm. Like Brother Solanus Casey he was assigned as doorkeeper at the little college where he had spent his novitiate. He held the job for forty years. His job description also included washing the floors and windows, carrying in the firewood and being a general gofer in running messages back and forth. Some were impressed by this simple man, others were not, especially his superior at the college, who seemed to have it in for Brother André and made him his constant whipping boy. It was a torturous cross that André bore valiantly. Still, his piety continued to grow. He would engage in long and devout prayer even during the night. He recited the rosary constantly.

All this time two scenarios began quietly to play out in André's life, one connected to the other. One was André's unflagging devotion to St. Joseph, perhaps because, like himself, Joseph was a hidden saint far from the spotlight. The other was that André would recommend St. Joseph to one and all so unceasingly that soon some people were claiming that through St. Joseph *and* Brother André they were being cured. Suddenly the miracles grew. They were astounding and many. Soon he became known as The Miracle Worker. St. Joseph and those miracles would mark Brother André's mission and life until he died. Cures and concomitant notoriety continued with a bewildered Brother André refusing to take any credit for these cures. All he wanted was to build a chapel to his patron.

No surprise that being dubbed as the miracle worker of Mt. Royal brought André a good deal of both admiration and criticism. The parents who sent their boys to the school where André worked, for example, were understandably not happy at all those diseased and needy people flocking in and out to see him. Some of the staff were jealous, and some anti-clerical doctors were furious at the "fake healer." Some referred to him as "the old fool on the mountain." The critics soon began complaining to his superiors and even to the public health officials. The bishop of Montreal dismissed the complaints but nevertheless felt it was time to have a chat with this man to see what he was all about. He met with Brother André and left impressed with his sincerity. Eventually so were the public health officials who had made an investigation of what went on at the college.

Brother André continued to dream of his chapel in honor of St. Joseph, a concept that had been suggested by others before him.

André never lost his fervor for it and even traveled to the United States to beg contributions. In 1896, the Congregation of the Holy Cross, fearing secular entrepreneurs would eventually move in and crowd them out, purchased the land. André's dream came true when, in 1924, the construction of Saint Joseph's Oratory on the side of a mountain began. It is and remains an impressive structure. It is situated on the mountain with long stairs to the ground. It is taller than St. Patrick's in New York or Notre Dame in Paris. It could hold the famed St. Paul's in London within its walls. Its cross can be seen for miles. Millions of people have flocked there to visit the shrine and the tomb of the lowly doorkeeper.

For all of his poor health, Brother André died in 1937, at the age of ninety-one. The name Saint Joseph was the last intelligible word he uttered in this life. If 20,000 passed by Brother Solanus' coffin, a million people filed past Brother André's. During that time the confessionals were filled with people, including some of his sworn enemies. He was beatified by Pope John Paul II in 1982, and made a saint by Pope Benedict XVI in 2010.

38

Oscar Romero

Oscar Romero was born on August 15, 1917, in a Salvadoran mountain town near the Honduran border, the second of seven children. His family was better off financially than many of their neighbors, but were still very poor. The Romeros had neither electricity nor hot running water, and the children slept on the floor. Since his parents could not afford to educate the bright lad beyond the age of twelve, they apprenticed him to a local carpenter although Oscar had dreams of becoming a priest. Eventually he entered the minor seminary in San Miguel at the age of thirteen and moved on to the national seminary in San Salvador. In recognition of his intellectual talents, he completed his studies at the Gregorian University in Rome (an incubation school for bishops). He was ordained in Rome in 1942.

Because of the priest shortage Fr. Romero was called home to El Salvador. On the way back he and a friend stopped off in Spain and in Cuba where, because he had come from fascist Italy, he was placed in an internment camp. After several months in prison Romero became sick, and some priests helped to have him transferred to a hospital, from which he was released and allowed to go back home. There he initially served as pastor of a rural parish and soon was moved up to the rectorship of the interdiocesan seminary and made secretary of the Diocese of San Miguel, a position he held for twenty-three years. One thing he long recognized before anyone else was the power of radio, and he began broadcasting his sermons to the poor people. He never ceased to take advantage of the radio. A rising star, he continued to work in administration serving as pastor of the cathedral parish of Santo Domingo, Executive Secretary of the Episcopal Council for Central America and Panama, and as editor of the archdiocesan newspaper.

In 1970, he became auxiliary bishop for the Archdiocese of San Salvador, assisting the elderly Archbishop Luis Chavez y Gonzalez who, deeply influenced by the Second Vatican Council, was implementing progressive reforms in pastoral work throughout the archdiocese. The conservative Romero was not happy or comfortable with several of the programs. He was glad to leave the archdiocese in 1974 to become Bishop of Santiago de Maria.

But no matter where he was, Bishop Romero could not escape the political ferment of the times. Popular resistance to economic and political oppression was growing as rapidly in Romero's diocese as in any other part of El Salvador. Although a few farm workers and laborers saw armed revolution as the only viable recourse, the vast majority turned to the social teachings of the Church. Thousands joined small Christian communities that sought to reform their society in the light of the Gospels.

But as so often happens the wealthy elites who had a stake in the inequality opposed all this. They ordered the military to shoot strikers, union organizers, and human rights activists, especially teachers, nuns, and priests. Mercenary death-squads roamed the countryside killing, raping, and torturing with impunity. Romero strenuously denounced violence against people who had "…taken to the streets in orderly fashion to petition for justice and liberty," just as he had denounced "…the mysticism of violence" being preached by the true revolutionaries. His words were not heeded. On June 21, 1975, Salvadoran National Guardsmen hacked five *campesinos* to death in the tiny village of Tres Calles. Romero rushed to the site to console the families and to offer Mass. That same day he wrote a letter of protest to Col. Arturo Armando Molina, head of the military dictatorship ruling the nation and denounced the attack to the local National Guard commander personally. The commander pointed his finger at the bishop and replied: "Cassocks are not bulletproof," the first but not the last death threat directed at Romero. During his two years as Bishop of Santiago de Maria, Romero crisscrossed his diocese on horseback, talking with laboring families to learn how he could best serve them. The reality of their lives horrified the bishop. Every day he discovered children dying because their parents could not pay for simple penicillin; people who were paid less than half of the legal minimum wage; people who had been savagely beaten for "insolence" after they asked for long overdue pay. Romero began using the resources of the diocese—and his own personal resources—to help the poor, but he knew that simple charity was not enough. In a pastoral letter released in November 1976, he wrote feelingly of the plight of the thousands of coffee plantation workers in his diocese. Some of his auxiliary bishops cautioned him that he was going a bit too far in defending the poor.

Nevertheless, he was still regarded as a conservative, especially in comparison to Archbishop Chavez, who had reached mandatory retirement age. Which is why the government, the military, and the aristocracy were delighted to see this quiet intellectual replace the retired Archbishop (the more liberal clergy were not). That sentiment was not to last. As Oscar Romero was being installed as Archbishop of San Salvador, El Salvador was on the brink of civil war. General Carlos Humberto Romero (no relation) proclaimed himself President of El Salvador following a blatantly fraudulent election. Eight days later, scores of people were killed when the police opened fire on thousands of demonstrators protesting election corruption. That same month, three foreign priests were beaten and expelled from the country, and a Salvadoran priest was abducted, beaten nearly to death, and thrown through the doors of the chancery. On March 12, 1977, a death squad ambushed Romero's dear friend, Fr. Rutilio Grande, SJ, killing him and the young boy who was giving Fr. Grande a ride to the rural church where he planned to celebrate Mass. Romero was shocked and saddened. "When I looked at Rutilio lying there dead," he said, "I thought, 'If they have killed him for doing what he did, then I too have to walk the same path.'" While he remained deeply saddened by the brutal murder he was also profoundly moved by the sugar-cane workers' testimony to Fr. Grande's works on their behalf and by their faith that Jesus would send them a new champion. That was Romero's turning point, his moment of conversion. Two days later in a Mass at San Salvador Cathedral, celebrated by a hundred priests before an immense crowd in the plaza, Romero called Grande and his two companions "…co-workers in Christian liberation" and he declared,

> the government should not consider a priest who takes a stand for social justice as a politician, or a subversive element, when he is fulfilling his mission in the politics of the common good.

Romero twice demanded that the President of El Salvador thoroughly investigate the murders but got stonewalled. He was convinced that the right-wing government was in collusion with the aristocrats who killed for personal gain. Realizing that his traditional reluctance to speak out on political matters had been a passive endorsement of repression and corruption he notified the president that representatives of the archdiocese would no longer appear with government leaders at public ceremonies. He also made the controversial decision to cancel Masses throughout the entire country the following Sunday, except for the one on the steps of the cathedral, to which the faithful of all parishes were invited. More than 100,000 people attended. The event drew sharp criticism from the government, the military, and some factions within the Church, but it united the population, and it clearly announced Romero's belated acceptance of Fr. Gustavo Gutierrez' dictum, "to know God is to do justice."

He brought these human rights abuses to the Vatican. He also wrote to President Jimmy Carter, appealing to him as a fellow Christian, to stop sending military aid to the Salvadoran government. His letter went unheeded. President Carter did suspend aid in 1980, after the murders of four churchwomen, but President Reagan resumed and greatly increased aid to the Salvadoran government. In all, US aid averaged $1.5 million per day for twelve years. Romero's pleas for international intervention were also ignored. To his dismay, so were his calls for solidarity with his fellow bishops, all but one of whom turned their backs on him. He continued to plead for an end to oppression, for reform of the nation's deeply institutionalized structures of social and economic injustice, and for simple Christian decency. The rightists' only response was an increase in the death threats against Romero, and fire-bombings of the archdiocese's newspaper and radio stations.

Four more priests were assassinated in 1979, along with many hundreds of catechists and delegates of the Word. The peasant death toll exceeded 3,000 per month. In all, at least 75,000–80,000 Salvadorans would be slaughtered; 300,000 would disappear and never be seen again; a million would flee their homeland; and an additional million would become homeless fugitives, constantly fleeing the military and police. All of this occurred in a nation of only 5.5 million people.

Romero had nothing left to offer his people except faith and hope. He continued to use his nationally broadcast Sunday sermons to report on conditions throughout the nation, to reassert the Church's prophetic and pastoral roles in the face of horrendous persecution, to promise his listeners that good would eventually come from evil and that they would not suffer and die in vain. On March 23, 1980, after reporting the previous week's deaths and disappearances, Romero began to speak directly to rank-and-file soldiers and policemen:

> Brothers, you are from the same people; you kill your fellow peasants…No soldier is obliged to obey an order that is contrary to the will of God…in the name of God, in the name of this suffering people, I ask you—I implore you—I command you in the name of God, stop the repression!

The answer came the following evening, while he celebrated a funeral Mass in the Chapel of Divine Providence Hospital. A paid assassin shot Archbishop Oscar Romero to death as he elevated the host and chalice before Communion. His blood spilled over the altar mingling with the contents of the chalice. Only moments before his death, he had reminded the mourners of the parable of wheat. His prophetic words:

> Those who surrender to the service of the poor through love of Christ will live like the grain of wheat that dies…The harvest comes because of the grain that dies…We know that every effort to improve society, above all when society is so full of injustice and sin, is an effort that God blesses, that God wants, that God demands of us.

More than 50,000 people gathered in the square outside San Salvador Cathedral to pay their last respects to Archbishop Romero on March 30, 1980. As they waved palm fronds and sang, "You are the God of the Poor," a series of small bombs were hurled into the crowd of mourners, apparently from the windows or balcony of the National Palace, which overlooks the Cathedral plaza, and cars on all four corners of the square exploded into flames. The blasts were followed by rapid volleys of gunfire that seemed to come from all four sides. Many witnesses saw army sharpshooters, dressed in civilian clothing, firing from the roof and balcony of the National Palace. An estimated 7,000 people took sanctuary inside the cathedral, which normally holds no more than 3,000. Many others were crushed against the security fence and closed gates that were intended to provide security for the funeral Mass. Cardinal Ernesto Corripto Ahumado, representative of Pope John Paul II at the funeral, was delivering his tribute to Archbishop Romero when the first bomb exploded. The service was immediately postponed as clerics tried in vain to calm the panicked crowd. As gunfire continued outside the cathedral, Romero's body was buried in a crypt below the sanctuary. The attack left forty mourners dead and hundreds seriously wounded.

Soon after Romero's death, El Salvador was plunged into a full-blown civil war that lasted for twelve years. The United Nations Truth Commission called the war "genocidal"—a war that claimed more than 75,000 lives, if one accepts the Salvadoran government's numbers, or more than three times that number if we accept the findings of most international investigating agencies.

On March 24, 2010, on the thirtieth anniversary of Romero's death, the Salvadorian president offered an official state apology for his assassination. In Rome, Romero's cause for canonization is advancing slowly. Right now he is listed as a "Servant of God" and will likely move to that of "Venerable." But for El Salvador he is and will always remain their unofficial patron saint, and for the rest of us a man who took the gospel seriously.

39

Maximilian Kolbe and the Foreman

This is a story told and witnessed to by a man named Ted Wojtkowski. Ted Wojtkowski considered himself an ordinary man. He came to Chicago from Poland after World War II. He worked as an engineer and raised a family. But as a young man Ted was a special witness to one of the great Good Shepherd heroes of the twentieth century. Go back to 1939.

In September of that year German tanks rumbled into Poland. The first village attacked by the Nazis was Wojtkowski home, He was then twenty years old. He went underground, manned a shortwave radio to gather war news from London, and secretly printed leaflets to let the villages know what was happening. Things gradually became too risky for him so he hopped on his father's bicycle and headed toward Hungary and then to France where he hoped to join the Polish army. But he was caught at the border, jailed, and then in May 1940 sent to the dreaded Auschwitz concentration camp.

Auschwitz was not yet a killing ground for Jews but a place for criminals and enemies and critics of the Nazi regime. Many priests were there. Wojtkowski lived in a two-story barracks with eight hundred other prisoners. He was sent out daily to build more barracks. The Nazis treated the prisoners cruelly, saving their special hatred and punishment for priests. Whenever a prisoner escaped, all the others had to stand in the sun for days with their hands on their heads. After a second escape, ten prisoners were machine-gunned. The third escape occurred around July 1941.

The punishment for this third infringement was that one hundred prisoners from Wojtkowski barracks were forced to stand in rows of ten. Ten of them would die. Wojtkowski stood in the eighth row. The camp commander ordered each row, one after another to step forward. He then began a random selection: one, two, three were pulled from each group. Wojtkowski hoped that the ten would already be picked before his the commander reached his row.

A fourth, fifth, and sixth man were picked. The sixth man broke down sobbing, "My wife, my children! Who will take care of them?" Suddenly a prisoner from the sixth row spoke up. He turned to the commander and said. "I will take the place of this man with the wife and children." Everyone looked. Wojtkowski in particular noticed that there was something serene and remarkable about the volunteer's demeanor. The commander, however, was not impressed. "You must be one of those vermin priests," he snarled. But he accepted him as one of the ten. All ten, this volunteer and the nine others, were locked in a bunker to starve to death. The Germans would not waste bullets on them.

That man, that volunteer, was indeed a priest. But he wasn't just any priest. He was the well-known Franciscan Father Maximilian Kolbe. He was a leader and a gifted man. He published religious magazines and newspapers read by more than one million Poles. He was widely admired, running the largest Catholic religious house in the world. Intensely devoted to the Blessed Mother, Kolbe supervised six hundred and fifty friars at an evangelization center near Warsaw. Naturally the Nazis regarded Kolbe with suspicion and mistrust after they invaded Poland. When he resisted pressure to apply for German citizenship, for which he was eligible, he was arrested on February 17, 1941.

Back to the incident. When the guards were out of earshot, the prisoners swapped information with one another about the fate of those ten men in the bunker starving to death. It tuned out that Kolbe was leading the doomed men in prayer and hymns. A piece of bread had been smuggled in to be used for Mass. After three weeks, all the men had died except Kolbe who was near death. The Nazis, impatient to use the bunker to punish others, had a doctor inject poison into Kolbe to finish him off.

The man Kolbe had saved, whose place he took, was but a poor anonymous peasant farmer. Kolbe, on the other hand, was a renowned man, only forty-seven, one of the most well-known and accomplished men in Poland. Yet he exchanged his life for the other. Truly a Good Shepherd And he saved not only that peasant but also Wojtkowski himself who, inspired by Kolbe's act, endured many years of backbreaking labor and abuse in the camp.

Finally, in 1945, while being force-marched to Dachau, Wojtkowski escaped and took refuge with a German priest who hid him and fed him until the Allies rolled into Germany. Wojtkowski finally got to the United States and moved to a Chicago suburb with a large Jewish population. He kept a scrapbook on Father Kolbe and a piece of his clothing and an original signature. A large painting of Kolbe hung in his study.

As for Maximillian Kolbe, he lived Christ's words, "Greater love than this no one has than to lay down his life for his friends."

Other anonymous heroes defined the darkness of Auschwitz. One survivor relates a story of when he was a fifteen-year-old prisoner there. He told of the lack of food and water, the unrelenting cold, the pain of not knowing whether his parents were still alive. He then tells of one snow-covered Christmas. He and the other prisoners were working as usual with the foreman watching them at every minute making sure that they were making every round of ammunition that was supposed to be made. And then, he says, the foreman called him over. He was sure he was going to be punished because while he was walking over to the foreman, the SS man in the background was whipping his whip. He knew that if you didn't work fast and didn't do the work like it was supposed to be done, they beat you.

He was fifteen and his legs were shaking as he approached pleading with the foreman not to hurt him, promising him he would work faster. And the foreman said bend down, bend down and the boy felt he is about to be beaten when the foreman says softly "take this white bread and put it under your coat and go out fast."

That, he realized, was his Christmas present. The SS man was behind the foreman, and he knew the foreman had bet his life to give a child a chance. He writes, "You know what a slice of white bread meant? Could you imagine that I am starving? Instead of beating me he gave me bread I could share with my sister. So you see, everywhere there are good people, everywhere." We call them saints.

40

St. Dad

Because, as I indicated in the Introduction, religious orders have the clout, time, and money to promote their saints, the calendar gets top heavy with priests, brothers, and nuns and this book reflects that. I have, however, tried to offset this with profiles of ordinary people ("Saintly Snapshots," chapter 22 and "Christmas Card Saints," chapter 23). Here, once more, I continue to check out the ordinary and I could find no more unsung and underappreciated ordinary saints than—our dads! I know it's a bold statement and one not in favor everywhere. Dads are pummeled in the popular press as selfish, mean-spirited, chauvinist slobs. The popular magazines even ask if their gender is needed. "Are Men Necessary?" is a headline reflecting the rise of single mothers and modern technology that appear to make dads obsolete.

But it's time to take a look at what some don't see or want to see: the power, the influence, and yes, even the holiness, of dads. To prove my point I turn to the late Tim Russert, the former Washington bureau chief of NBC News. Before his unexpected and sudden death, he wrote a book about his father called *Big Russ & Me*. It was a huge success and soon became number one on the *New York Times* best-seller list. This book about fathers clearly struck a chord all across America. People resonated with the father-son story. The book's success seemed to be a refutation of some radical feminists who dismiss fathers as unnecessary and useless in spite of social science still consistently and overwhelmingly pointing out the need for fathers and the high correlation between delinquency, crime, and antisocial behavior and fatherless children, especially boys.

Tim Russert knew this personally and academically. Early on in his career he worked for Senator Daniel Patrick Moynihan, and through him became aware of the effect of missing fathers on the larger society. Back in 1965, while working in the Johnson administration, Senator Moynihan had written a report called "The Negro Family: The Case for National Action." In it he described the ongoing breakup of black families in large part due to absent fathers. The nation was shocked to learn that twenty-four percent of black children were born into single-parent families. Five decades later, that number has reached seventy percent, and figures for the Hispanic and white communities have shown similar upward trends. Russert says that he talked about this with Charles Barkley, one of the NBA's best-known and most outspoken players. Barkley, who grew up without a father, pointed out that the lack of financial support is only part of the problem, and that a boy needs a dad for another, more basic reason: to learn how to become a man. As he put it, "You don't know how to be a man unless somebody teaches you."

Tim then goes on to say something that pertains to saints. He says that he received close to sixty thousand letters and e-mails and that most of the letters described a father's sacrifice, fortitude, and perseverance. They told of his advice and guidance; or gave examples of his kindness, generosity, love, and, yes, wisdom. Many of the letters were unforgettable. Moreover, Russert notes, these letters and stories—which he included in a new book, *Wisdom of Our Fathers*—have strikingly two things in common.

First, he says, the letters he received are overwhelmingly positive even though there was the occasional dissenting voice telling of a bad father. No, in exceedingly large numbers his correspondents admired their fathers and deeply cherished their memories. The second big theme that comes across in these letters, Russert says, is that the most precious things a father can provide are time, attention, and love. "For about six months I read hundreds of e-mails and letters every day, but I can't recall a single one that said, 'My father gave me every material thing I wanted,' or, 'What I remember most about my dad is the new TV he bought me.'" What we remember about our fathers, Russert says, "has little or nothing to do with material objects. We remember the time they gave us— whether indirectly (through hard work) or in more conventional ways—time spent providing advice, telling a bedtime story, or simply showing up for a recital, a spelling bee, or an athletic event."

So, here's some random sample letters from his book, *Wisdom of Our Fathers*. Read and savor them and think of your own father. This man writes:

> "One thing I'll never forget about my father—a hard-as-nails tough-love man who fought in two world wars and a war in Africa during the twenties—was the single tear running down his cheek the day he dropped me off at Fort Dix on my way to Vietnam, and the one hug that made up for twenty-two years of no hugging. Only he could understand what the coming year had in store for me He couldn't even share his sorrow with my mother. Because of her weak heart we told her I was going to a missile base in Guam. It seemed as if all the year of absence from each other's lives came together at that moment in New Jersey. We finally shared a bond no one else in my family could ever understand, father to son, man to man, soldier to soldier."

Another:

> "As a young child, I sometimes stuttered. Once, when I was six and our family was traveling in the car, I was

trying to tell my parents something and couldn't get the words out. Stuttering confused me, which caused me to stutter even more. Although this didn't happen very often, it was painful for my parents to witness. That day, while my dad was driving, he calmly reached into the backseat and pulled me closer to him. Then he put his arm around my shoulders and patted my right arm. I remember feeling a sense of immediate calm that allowed me to get the words out."

This one wrote:

"I loved my dad very much, but I really didn't know him. My two brothers and I were put in an orphanage at a very young age because he couldn't take care of us. We were allowed visitors once a month, and I remember sitting on the front steps, my eyes glued on that long driveway, hoping that my dad would show up. And he did. He lived in Louisville, six miles away, and he walked six miles to visit us because he couldn't afford the bus fare. But he always brought some kind of little toy. He was buried in Shepherdsville, Kentucky. I am seventy-three now, but someday I hope to go there and see his grave. To this day I can't talk about my dad without getting choked up."

This one wrote:

"A few weeks after Dad was buried, I was going through his personal effects. I opened his wallet, where I found a dollar and a couple of pictures of his four grand-daughters. I pulled out his driver's license and out fell a tag like the ones you get on your Christmas gifts. I looked at it closely and, on the back, written in my mother's hand, was a note that said, "He tried to write his name and he wanted to ask you, 'When are you coming home, Daddy?' This man whom I used to think I could never satisfy, had carried around for forty-seven years a note from his wife and two-year old son from Christmas, 1944. I learned from this that a father's love is an enduring thing. Sometimes, it's hard for children to see and sometimes it's harder for fathers to show, but that love is always there."

Another writes,

"In the summer of 1968, I had just graduated from high school in Brooklyn and was eagerly awaiting the start of a college career at Brooklyn College in September. I got a summer job doing clerical work at a shipping company and made sixty dollars a week before taxes. When I told my father about the job, he was excited for me and added that he wanted me to contribute fifteen dollars a week for the household expenses. I was angry at him for asking me to give up some of my hard-earned money, but I complied with his request every week. The week before I started college, he handed me a large envelope that contained all the money I had given him over the summer. 'I wasn't interested in your money,' he told me. 'I just wanted to teach you a little responsibility.' And he did."

And a few short ones:

"My dad taught me to tie my shoes, to cross the street, to get an education, and to believe in my country, my

God and my family. I never had to look far for my hero. He was just across the living room, sitting in his favorite chair, reading the newspaper and watching the nightly news. Dad's been gone three years now, but I still think of him every day, the way he would laugh at a joke so hard that he'd start to cry, or how, when we were little, he'd get up in the morning, come down for breakfast and remind us to say good morning to Mr. Sun. All these years later, I finally realized he *was* the sun."

And this:

"A couple of years ago, I called to congratulate my parents on their fifty-third wedding anniversary. And I complimented them on how much their marriage had meant to their children. As I was shedding a tear, Dad said, "That's a load of baloney. The deal between your mother and me was that whoever left first had to take all eight of you!"

Another light note:

"When we were about ten and twelve, my brother and I decided it was time to start smoking. But where would we hide the cigarettes? We found a loose board in the attic. Just the place, we thought. After all, nobody would smell smoke coming from the attic. Two sons of a volunteer fireman smoking in the attic! Dumb and dumber! One evening, we decided it was time for a break in homework and a well-earned smoke, but much to our surprise—and horror—the loose floorboard was nailed shut. Nothing was ever said or needed to be said. And we never smoked cigarettes again."

Let me end with one that says it all:

"I was visiting my parents a few years after my mother's health started failing, when my dad had completely taken over her care and the house. I was up early and heard them talking. I didn't want to disturb the moment, and I tried not to listen, but I overheard my mother tell Dad that she was sorry she was such a poor companion these days. She wanted to be traveling and doing things together, as they had often discussed. There was silence and then Dad said, in a choked voice, 'Don't you know I just want to be in the same room with you?'

"I was struck by the simplicity and love in that remark... I loved my parents for the example of their relationship. My mother died several years ago, Dad is still alive, but he is suffering from some dementia. He lives with me now, and I have come to understand the simplicity and importance of being in the same room with him."

If their children found something special in their fathers, if through them they caught a glimpse of what God might be like, then who is to say they were not saints?

Let me end by citing another author, Philip Yancey. In his book, *Disappointment with God*, he relates a touching story from his own life.

One time on a visit to his mother—who had been widowed years earlier, in the month of Philip's first birthday—they spent the afternoon together looking through a box of old photos. A certain picture of him as an eight-month-old baby caught his eye. Tattered and bent, it looked too banged up to be worth keeping, so he asked her why, with so many other better pictures of him at the same age, she had kept this one. Yancey writes, "My mother explained to me that she had kept the photo as a memento, because during my father's illness it had been fastened to his iron lung."

During the last four months of his life, Yancey's father lay on his back, completely paralyzed by polio at the age of twenty-four, encased from the neck down in a huge, cylindrical breathing unit. With his two young sons banned from the hospital due to the severity of his illness, he had asked his wife for pictures of her and their two boys. Because he was unable to move even his head, the photos had to be jammed between metal knobs so that they hung within view above him--the only thing he could see. The last four months of his life were spent looking at the faces he loved.

Philip Yancey writes, "I have often thought of that crumpled photo, for it is one of the few links connecting me to the stranger who was my father. Someone I have no memory of, no sensory knowledge of, spent all day, every day thinking of me, devoting himself to me, loving me. The emotions I felt when my mother showed me the crumpled photo were the very same emotions I felt one February night in a college dorm room when I first believed in a God of love. Someone like my father is there, I realized. Someone is there everyday thinking of me, loving me. It was a startling feeling of wild hope, a feeling so new and overwhelming that it seemed fully worth risking my life on."

The contagion of saints. The contagion of our fathers.

LEGENDS
AND
FABLES

LEGENDS: AN EXCURSUS

Legends go way back to the dawn of antiquity. They were a staple of the ancient world. It is no surprise then that, when Christians appeared on the scene, they tended to imitate the old stories, and many Christian legends were often Christianized pagan tales. As such they frequently repeated the favorite theme of the hero having power over nature—a much wished-for fantasy because antiquity's context was not only farming, fishing, and hunting but also earthquakes, storms, plagues, freaks of nature, herbs, alchemy, and a lack of scientific explanations. Anyone who had the power to control these things was indeed a hero, and if actual heroes were in short supply, the imagination provided. So it's no surprise that the Christian saint also became a kind of lord of the elements: King Canute held back the waves, Tolstoy's bishop walked on the waters, St. Teresa of Avila levitated, St. Raymond of Pentefore flew, Jerome cowered the lion.

The earliest Christian saints were those impressive and heroic martyrs of the first centuries and the desert fathers of the centuries following. Their lives were often embellished with the deeds and trappings of the ancient heroes, and this explains the sometime similarities between the gods and the saints. And if the ancient gods were in charge of the different departments of life—the god of fertility, the god of war, the god of the winds, and so on, the saints, known as patron saints, were likewise assigned their area of expertise: the patron saint of tailors, shoemakers, lawyers, lost articles, and the rest. In the early and later Middle Ages, stories and books appeared about saints that reflected the concerns of the day: the savior saints appeared in times of war and pillage, mystical saints in monastery times, Mary in cathedral times, Sacred Host stories in Corpus Christi times (the feast was first celebrated throughout the Church in 1264). Later on, scholars tried to separate the facts from the fictions, and this scholarly work continues to our day, which is why we had St. Philomena deleted and St. Christopher downsized.

Given this background, why do I include the legends of the saints here? They are not particularly in vogue in our one-dimensional society. Today our modern mentality may enjoy them as entertainment but it does not permit us to plumb them as truth. So why bother? Because among storytellers there is this old adage: "Some stories are factual, all stories are true." To help you grasp this, let me share some words from author, Joan Windham, who wrote a wonderfully delightful Lives of the Saints for children. She notes in her preface:

> Most of the things I have written about really did happen to the Saints, but some of the things I have written about are just Stories that people tell about them, and these Stories are called Legends. All the Legends could have happened if God wanted it that way, and that, I think, is how most of them got started. If the Saint was a Gardening kind of a man, there are Gardening Legends about him. If he was a man who lived in a Starving place then there are Legends about plenty of Food arriving very surprisingly…. And so, in this way, we find out what kind of person the Saint was, as well as what kind of things he did, by reading Legends about him.

And then she adds:

> I'll tell you something…There is a legend about me. In
> my garden is a pond and once I dropped a trowel into
> it and I nearly fell in when I was fishing it out. A very
> little boy thought I had fallen in and every time he
> sees the pond he says, "Aunt Joan fell in there!" And
> the other people hear him, and although it was some
> time ago now, a good many people describe exactly
> what they think happened and how wet I was and how
> there were water lilies round my neck and all kinds of
> other stories! But they all believe that I really did fall
> into the pond. I didn't but it is just the sort of thing
> that I might have done!

So what's she saying is that even though the stories about
her falling into the pond are not factual, they may well be true in
the sense that they tell a great deal about her, the kind of person
she is.

So when we pick up a book like this one containing a few legends of the saints we must be aware that not everything there is
literal—all stories by definition expand, and the lives of the saints
more so—but everything is historical. That is, to return to Joan
Windham, she really did historically exist. She did not literally fall
into the pond but, as she said, it's characteristic of her. Maybe not
about her sister or brother or husband, but everyone who knew
her would readily comment, "Whether she actually fell into the
pond or not, that would be just like dear Joan, just the sort of thing
she would do!" So, we now have a capsule of her, about her personality "type," if you will. We have an insight into her, the kind of
person she is, what we can expect of her and the things that would
be consistent with who she is. As she wrote: "And so in this way,

we find out about the kind of a person the Saint was, as well as the kind of things he did, by reading Legends about him."

That's the way it is with legends: they conceal a truth. So let us proceed starting off with one of Joan Windham's stories, a child's view of the Seven Capital Sins.

41

The Legend of St. Alexander

Once upon a time there was a forest in Rumania, there lived in the forest a man called Alexander, and people sometimes called him Alex for short. Alexander was a Charcoal Burner and he used to collect little twigs and thin branches from the trees in the forest and he made little fires and burned the sticks very slowly so that they turned into black sticks called Charcoal. People use charcoal for quite a lot of things. They draw with it, and make fires with it, and use it for medicine, and make shoe polish with it. So you can see what a useful job Alexander had. So Alexander looked after his little fires by himself all day and he learned to be very Patient because if he was Impatient his charcoal would turn into ashes. All this made him think how quiet and patient God must be.

While Alexander was quietly living in the forest and burning his charcoal and thinking about God and watching the Birds and Animals there were great Goings On in the town where he sold his charcoal. And this is what was happening: At first there had been very few Christians in the town, but as time went on there were more and more until at last the priest said that they really ought to have a Bishop of their own instead of belonging to a Bishop called Gregory who lived a very long way off and scarcely ever had time to come and see them. So it was decided that Bishop Gregory should come and that everybody should say which priest they wanted to be the new Bishop. Well, some wanted This Priest and some wanted That Priest and some didn't know whom they wanted but they didn't want either of Those. At last they collected seven priests who wanted to be the Bishop and they wrote and told Gregory that they wanted him to come and choose.

The Town Hall was all ready with a Throne at the end of it for Bishop Gregory and chairs and seats for all the people. When everyone was settled the First man who might be the Bishop came in. He was tall and thin with a big nose and a very Grand expression. He looked at the crowds of people as if they were too Common for Words. The people who wanted him to be the Bishop clapped and cheered as he went and stood in front of Gregory. "Do you think that you would be a good Bishop ?" asked Gregory. "I am sure I would," said the man. "I think that you are too Proud," said Gregory. "Next please!"

The Second man had silk clothes and a jeweled crucifix, and he had a rosary made of real rubies in his hand. "Would you keep all those lovely things for your self, if you were the Bishop?' asked Gregory. "Of course I should. They are my own property," said the man, and he held them a little tighter. "You are too Covetous, I think," said Gregory. (Covetous is selfish and miserly.) "Next please!" said Gregory.

The Third man had the gayest coloured clothes and a smiling face and beautiful curly hair. He winked at all the people and the ladies clapped their hands because he was so handsome. "Do you want people to go on thinking that you are handsome and clever when you are the Bishop?" asked Gregory. "But of course!" said the man, and he looked quickly at the people to see if they were listening. "Even a Bishop must have his bit of fun." "I think that you are too fond of Pretty Ladies," said Gregory. "Next please!"

The Fourth man had black hair and a frowning face. He stared at the people angrily and then went and stood in front of Gregory. The people who wanted him clapped for him but he shook his head at them and they stopped. "If you were the Bishop, would you be Strict with the people and punish them severely if they broke the rules?" asked Gregory. "I would," said the man. "They are a lazy, sinful lot, but I'd not put up with any of their nonsense!" And he glared at Gregory. "You get Angry too easily," said Gregory. "Next, please!"

The Fifth man was very fat indeed, but he looked kindly at the people and he waved his hand at the ones who wanted him. As he stood in front of Gregory he pulled a buttered bun out of his pocket and began to eat it. "Excuse me!" he said. "Couldn't you have waited until after the Choosing before you ate your bun?" asked Gregory. "Not me!" said the man, "I wouldn't miss my tea for any man on earth. It keeps a man good tempered to be fat." "I think that you are too Greedy," said Gregory. "Next please!"

The Sixth man was thin and mean looking. He did not look happy. He stared at all the priests who had already seen Gregory. (They were standing at the back of the Throne and waiting to see who would be Chosen.) "Well," said Gregory, "what is the matter? Aren't you happy? Don't you want to be Bishop after all?" "No good me wanting," said the man. "I've no good looks like that man over there, or riches like that one, or a nice house like that one, or a kind family like that one. I never get the things that Other People have." "You are too Envious to be happy," said Gregory. (Envious is being so jealous of other people's things that you haven't time to see what nice things you have yourself.) "Next please!" said Gregory. But no one came.

"Next please!" said Gregory, looking around. "I though that you said that there were seven people who wanted to be Bishop," he whispered to the Mayor who was standing beside him, "I've only seen six." "NEXT PLEASE!!" shouted the Mayor, and all the people laughed. Then the door banged and in came an untidy man with ruffled hair and his shoes undone. He was yawning and rubbing his eyes.

"Sorry, my Lord," he said to Gregory. "As I was the last one I thought that I'd have a nap while I was waiting and I didn't hear you call."

"Do you always have naps when you can?" asked Gregory.

"Always, my Lord," said the man solemnly, "a man can't have too much sleep, I always say."

"I think that you are too Lazy," said Gregory.

All the people rustled and coughed and sat up and shuffled their feet. They stared at Gregory and waited for him to say which of the seven priests would be the Bishop. "Well," said Gregory, and he looked round at all the people, "I am sorry but I don't think that any of them would do for a Bishop."

The people started talking among themselves and then someone shouted: "But we must have one of them! There isn't any one else!" "No," said Gregory. "They may not be so bad as ordinary people go but they're no good for Bishops." All the people started arguing again, and in the noise Gregory said to God: "Please, God, if you really want a Bishop here, will you choose one for yourself? It is very difficult for me with all these seven, and the people are getting so cross." Just then someone shouted: "You'd better have Alexander the Charcoal Burner if you can't think of anyone better!"

All the people laughed because they couldn't imagine having sooty, raggy Alexander for a Bishop! But Gregory knew that this was God's answer to his prayer and so he held up his hand for the people to stop laughing and said: "Who is this Alexander?" "I was only joking," said the man who had shouted. "He is a Charcoal Burner and he lives in the forest." "Will somebody please go and get him?" said Gregory. The people all stared. What was Gregory thinking about? Did he really mean to see if Alexander would do? Yes, he did.

So Alexander was brought along. First he washed the black Marks off his face and hands, then he went to Bishop Gregory and knelt and kissed his ring. Then he stood up and waited to see why the Bishop had sent for him. "Alexander," said Gregory, "do you think that you would be a good Bishop?" "Me, my Lord?" said Alexander, "No, I have no learning. I don't know anything at all." "Would you like a Rosary made of Rubies?" "Why no, thank you, my Lord," said Alexander, "I have a very nice wooden one; it will last me my lifetime."

"Do you like Parties and Pretty Ladies?" "I don't know any," said Alexander. "I've never been asked to a Party myself but a bit of fun now and then is good for everybody." He wondered why Gregory was asking him all these questions in front of the townspeople. "Do you think that the Townspeople are a lazy sinful lot?" asked Gregory. "Oh no, my Lord, please don't think that! There's good in everyone if you look for it." Alexander had quite forgotten how mean the people were in paying for their charcoal. "Have you had your Tea yet?" asked Gregory. "I don't have it as a rule," said Alexander, "only when it is raining and I can't burn my charcoal. I eat when I am hungry and that does me nicely." "Are you happy?" asked Gregory. "Have you everything that you want?" "I'm very happy, my Lord," said Alexander. "I love my work, I have enough to eat, I have my own little house and God is good to me." "Would you change your work for something quite different?" asked Gregory. "I would if God wished it," said Alexander.

Gregory stood up. He walked down the steps of his throne and put his arm round Alexander's shoulders. "Here is your new Bishop," he said to the people. At first they all sat with their mouths open. Surely it could not be true! Surely the Bishop was having a joke with them!

Then, as they began to think, they saw that Alexander was just the opposite to all the other seven, and they looked at Alexander. And looking at him they loved him. So Alexander the Charcoal Burner became a Bishop and he was one for years and years but in the end he was a Martyr. St. Alexander's Special Day is on August 11.

42

The Legend of Abbot Makarios

Once upon a time, Abbot Makarios, a holy monk, was caught up into seventh heaven and talked with Jesus. When he returned to earth he was radiant and his disciples knew something unusual had happened, that he had had a vision of the Lord. So right away they were pressing him, "What went on? What went on? What did you talk about?"

"Well," said Abbot Makarios serenely, one of the things the Master told me was that I am going to enter the Kingdom of Heaven. And, not only that, but I am going to sit at the main banquet table right next to the Lord himself!" The disciples were ecstatic to know that their Master, the Holy Monk, Abbot Makarios, would be sitting right next to the Lord Jesus in the Kingdom because, as is well known, all Masters took their disciples with them. So naturally they were overjoyed, but also, at the same time, they were anxious. "This is not going to happen soon?" they asked. "No," smiled Abbot Makarios, "I don't think it's going to be for a while. You don't have to worry."

Nevertheless, as the days went by, Abbot Makarios began to wonder about certain things. More specifically, he wondered that, if he was going to be at the Grand Banquet sitting on one side of the Lord, who was going to be sitting on the other side for all eternity? Not, mind you, that he thought he would get bored talking to the Lord—but, still—still he wondered, who would be sitting on the other side?

After a while he became quite obsessed with the issue and began asking Jesus who it would be. In the beginning, the Lord was not overjoyed with this question and simply said, "You don't need to know." But Abbot Makarios kept hammering and hammering at him until at last he said, "OK, OK, I'll tell you who it is." So he gave Abbot Makarios his name, the name of another monk, a hermit who lived far away. He in turn told his disciples and, for the next few months, they spent all their time tracking down this man. And as soon as they found out where he lived, the disciples told Abbot Makarios, and Abbot Makarios decided he would go and visit him. And he would go during the Great Holy Week so they could celebrate the great mysteries together.

Well, it was a stormy night and it was getting dark and it was getting colder than expected. He found the house and he knew the man was home because smoke was coming out of the chimney. Abbot Makarios knocked on the door very loudly and listened. Not a sound. Nobody came to the door. He rapped again and shouted.

"Let me in! Let me in!" Nothing. Then he heard some grunts behind the door, but nothing that sounded like a human being. He rapped on the door again and said, "I am a monk, an abbot! Easter is coming. Already the darkness is setting in. You must let me in!"

With that the door opened and Abbot Makarios beheld one of the biggest men he had ever seen. The man filled the whole doorway and had to bend to get out. He had a ragged beard and he was huge. Abbot Makarios had to squeeze himself in the doorway to get in and when he got in he noticed that the hut was very barren. It had a table and a chair and a bed, but nothing else except big cupboards and boxes of stuff. He said, "Are you Brother so-and-so?" The man replied, "Yeah." "Well," said Abbot Makarios, "I am also a monk, an abbot, the head of a monastery, and I have come to visit you." The huge Monk said, "I know who you are." "Well, aren't you going to invite me in for Holy Week?" The Huge Monk said, "No. I don't celebrate Holy Week."

This shocked Abbot Makarios. He thought to himself, "This man is so holy that he is going to sit next to me in the Heavenly Banquet forever—but he doesn't celebrate Holy Week? This is interesting." And he said out loud, "Well, I'm going to. Do you want to join me?" The big monk said, "No. You can do what you want." So Abbot Makarios took out the missal, lit the candles, brought out the bread and wine and began to celebrate Mass for Holy Thursday. Meanwhile, the other monk began to eat his meal. He opened up a cupboard and took out food. He opened up boxes and took out food. He laid the food on the bed, on the chairs, on the table, offering nothing to Abbot Makarios, and started stuffing himself. He ate everything in sight and he ate for hours. Finally, Abbot Makarios realized that if he was going to eat at all, he was going to have to take it. So he grabbed a little here and a little there, enough to keep body and soul together.

After they were finished and began putting away what was left, the Huge Monk suddenly said, "O.K., you've eaten. Now, get out. Get away. Go!" Abbot Makarios exclaimed, "But you can't get rid of me. This is Holy Thursday. You have to leave me here till at least two more days, Easter." "Well, all right," said the Huge Monk. "Find yourself a place to sleep." And with that he plopped himself down on his bed and went to sleep. Abbot Makarios watched him a while and then thought to himself, "Sometimes, you know, there are hidden saints who are so holy that they hide their holiness and their devotion from the rest of the people, They usually pray all night in the dark, doing penance for the world. Maybe he's going to get up while I'm asleep and spend the whole night in prayer. I'll just pretend I'm asleep and I'll watch."

So all night long Abbot Makarios struggled to stay awake seeing what the man would do, but all that he did was snore very loudly, turn over, whomp the pillow, and bang the wall. Abbot Makarios did not get much sleep, but the monk seemed to do pretty well. The next morning, the Huge Monk got up and the first thing he said was, "Get out!" Abbot Makarios protested, "I can't leave. It's Good Friday. I can't go till tomorrow, the Easter vigil." Well, there was a repeat for breakfast. Food came out of everywhere and the other monk stuffed himself again. Same thing at lunch and dinner and the next day as well. Nothing was offered to Abbot Makarios.

At this point he was definitely having second thoughts. This man was a clod. He was crude, rude, ignorant. He didn't keep Holy Week, didn't fast, didn't pray. He felt he had wasted his time in coming. This couldn't be the man who would be sitting next to him at the Heavenly Banquet forever. Did he misunderstand the Lord? No, he didn't think so. So he was beginning to wonder about the Lord, that he would make these kinds of decisions. But why? He, Abbot Makarios, deserved better than this. After all, he was the head of a monastery. He kept Holy Week. He fasted. He prayed. He observed the Holy Rule. He had devoted followers and he spoke with the Lord. But this other man, this huge oaf, was clearly an inferior breed, ill mannered, selfish, and, worst of all, a non-observant monk. In short, a sinner.

Thank heaven, Holy Saturday came and the vigil was over and Abbot Makarios was about to leave—and gladly at that. He was anxious to get away from such an inferior human being. He spoke to the huge monk. He said, "I came here because the Lord told me—and he told me very clearly—that you are going to sit next to me at the Heavenly Banquet forever." "Oh, yeah?" said the Huge Monk, "That's only if you believe that there *is* a Heavenly Banquet that lasts forever!" That was too much for Abbot Makarios and confirmed his worst suspicions. He stepped back from the brother so he wouldn't be contaminated, held his ears, raised his eyes to heaven, and exclaimed, "Enough! Enough! I'm going. But I need to ask you before I leave. Why do you live this way? Why do you not pray as I do? Why do you not celebrate Holy Week? And, most of all, why do you stuff yourself every day?"

There was a long silence. Then the huge monk looked at him with tears in his eyes and he said, "I'll tell you why. When I was very young, six or seven years old, I lived with my parents and my grandparents and my great grandparents. And we were very simple. We farmed our land and did what we could. And then the Infidels came. They burned everything to the ground. They destroyed the fields. They killed everyone. I watched them slaughter my mother, my father, my brothers, my sisters. The only ones they missed were my old grandfather and me. They left us with nothing, even though we had begged God for mercy. We had been good Christians."

He said, "We lived as best we could. We cleared a plot of land that had been burned. We started to plant and to try to put our lives back together again. Every morning after we planted, my grandfather would send me to the stream and I would bring back water. It was only two or three years after this that the Infidels came again. It seems they come in every generation at least once or twice to burn us out. But I was hiding in the bushes because I was bringing water back from the stream. And they got my grandfather, and they tied him to a tree and tried to make him blaspheme Jesus. And he wouldn't. He was a tiny wisp of a man, with straggly hair and poor—like the rest of us. And they threatened to kill him if he didn't blaspheme Jesus Christ. But he refused, praying aloud. And so they poured kerosene on him, and they lit him, and they watched him go up in flames. And I watched my grandfather. He went up so quick! Just like a flicker of a candle and he was out. And from that day forward, I swore to myself that when they came again—and they will—they'd find somebody who was so big and so fat that when they tied me to a tree and poured kerosene over me and lit me, I would burn so long, and so hot, and the fire would be so great, that they and the whole surrounding area would know that Jesus Christ has a witness and that God is still served."

And, as the tears continued to run down his face, the huge monk started to pray, "O Lord Jesus, Master of all, how long will you let your children kill each other?" And as the man continued to pray, Abbot Makarios started to inch his way out the door. As he closed the door softly behind him and listened to the man continuing to pray, for the first time in his life, Abbot Makarios wondered whether he was worthy to sit at the table at the Heavenly Banquet next to that man.

43

The Legend of St. Dismas

Jesus was crucified between two thieves, a nameless good thief and a nameless bad one. The bad one mocks Jesus and tells him to save himself and them. The good thief rebukes him and then, turning to Jesus, says, "Lord, remember me when you come into your kingdom." And Jesus promises paradise that very day.

Thus the wonderful core truth of last minute redemption and mercy. Still, it is rather an intriguing story. People pondered: it's too bad we don't know more about those two thieves. Were they Clint Eastwood characters or Tony Soprano types? Butch Cassidy and Sundance? How did they become that way? Where were they from? It drove the early Christians crazy until around the year 600 an apocryphal book appeared called *The Arabic Gospel of the Infancy of Our Savior.*

The book covers Mary and Joseph's escape journey into Egypt with the Christ Child. As Mary and Joseph are wandering through Egypt, looking for some place to call home, at least temporarily, the locals warn them about a certain stretch of desert that was teeming with robbers. Hoping to pass this stretch unnoticed, Mary and Joseph decide to travel by night. But it's no time at all when they come upon two highwaymen blocking the road ahead of them. The highwaymen, the robbers, in this apocryphal gospel, are named Dismas and Gestas.

Gestas is ready to get down to business and rob the Holy Family, but Dismas intervenes. "Let these persons go free," he says, "so that our comrades (who were sleeping nearby) may not see them." A strange request from a hardened criminal; Gestas dismisses it out of hand. So Dismas ups the ante. He says to Gestas, "Look, take these forty drachmas from me instead" and he tosses in his valuable belt as well. The drachmas and the belt are an offer Gestas can't refuse, so he stands aside and lets the Holy Family go, free and unmolested.

So now comes the tie-in. Before they continue on their way, Mary prophesies to Dismas, "I promise you, because of your kindness, the Lord God will sustain you and will grant you remission of your sins." And a very precocious Christ Child adds an aside, "Thirty years hence, O my mother, these two robbers will be raised upon the cross along with me, Dismas on my right hand, and Gestas on my left: and after that day, Dismas shall go before me into paradise."

Now we can imagine how it all began and we feel more satisfied. Legend that this is, it has become an acceptable story because it has kept the core truth in focus, the focus on mercy, forgiveness, and love. If you want a quick P.S., at some point—*when* is hard to pinpoint—Dismas segued into *Saint* Dismas, and he eventually became the patron saint of thieves in particular and criminals in general.

An example. There is a priest named Father Emil Kapaun from Kansas. He is being promoted for sainthood. He was a military chaplain during the Korean War. In November 1950 the North Koreans captured him and 1,200 American fighting men.

The American POWs got so little food they were on the verge of starvation, so every night Father Kapaun crept out of the barracks to steal corn, millet, and soybeans from the guards' storehouse to feed the soldiers. Being a good Christian, before Father Kapaun went out to steal, he prayed to St. Dismas, the Good Thief.

Thus in this instance, the initial true event of Calvary fleshes out into legends that in turn spill over into stories that in turn inspire new ways of forgiveness and compassion. Unravel the legends of the saints and you'll find a gospel truth.

44

The Legend of St. Christopher

• FORMER SAINT •

Christopher was a mild and gentle giant of a man who served the king of Canaan faithfully. Though he cared deeply for his lord, the king, he dreamed of serving the strongest master in the world.

Taking leave of Canaan, he traveled until he came to the castle of the one said to be the greatest ruler in the world. When the king saw the size and strength of Christopher, he made him second in command and invited him to dwell in his court.

One day when a minstrel was entertaining the king, he sang a song about the devil. Whenever the name of the devil was mentioned, the king made the sign of the cross. Christopher asked the king about his actions. "It is to ward off the devil," the king answered. "Do you fear his power?" asked Christopher. "Ah, yes," said the king. He has great might." Christopher shook his head sadly. "I must leave you, my lord, for I have a great desire to serve the most powerful one in this world. It seems the devil is that one."

Christopher began his search for the devil, wandering until he met a great company of knights. The leader of the knights, a man who appeared cruel and horrible, approached him and asked him what he wanted. "I am in search of the devil to be my master," said Christopher evenly. "I am the one you seek," said the terrible knight. Christopher immediately bowed before the devil and promised his allegiance.

A bit later, as the company of knights walked together, they came upon a cross standing at an intersection. Immediately the devil turned to the side, taking his followers in a circuitous route until he finally came back to the highway. "Why did we take this route?" asked Christopher. At first the devil was reluctant to answer, but Christopher persisted. "There was once a man called Christ who was killed on a cross," the devil explained. "When I see his sign, I am afraid and attempt to avoid it." "Then he is greater and more powerful than you," said Christopher. "I see that I have yet to find the one who is the greatest lord on the earth. I will leave you to find Christ, whoever he is."

Christopher began a long search for the one people called Jesus, the Christ. At last he came upon a pious hermit who welcomed him and began to teach him about Jesus. One day the hermit spoke to Christopher. "You are not ready to serve Christ. In order to do this you must fast." Christopher said, "It is most difficult for me to fast. Ask me to do something else." "You must wake early in the morning and pray long hours each day," the hermit said. "Please," said Christopher, "find me a task more to my ability. I am not a man who can pray for long periods of time."

The hermit thought for a moment before he spoke again. "You are indeed tall and strong. You shall live by the river and carry across anyone who comes in need. In that way you will serve Jesus. I hope that our Lord Christ will one day show himself to you." So Christopher began his life of service at the river, where the current was strong. There, with the help of a huge pole, he carried rich and poor alike over the treacherous river.

One day as he slept in his lodge by the river, Christopher heard the voice of child calling, "Christopher, come carry me over." When he looked outside, he saw no one. Back in his lodge, he again heard the voice call. Again his search was unsuccessful. The third time he went outside, he found a child who begged Christopher to carry him over the river. The giant took the child on his shoulders and began his walk across the river. As the water rushed against his body, the weight of the child was almost too much to bear. The farther he walked, the more the water swelled and the heavier the child rested on his shoulders. For the first time in his life, the giant Christopher was gripped with a fear of death.

At last, using all his might, Christopher reached land and put the child down. Lying nearly exhausted, Christopher spoke to the child. "I was in great trouble in the water. I felt as if I had the weight of the whole world on my shoulders." Then the child spoke. "Indeed you have borne a great burden, Christopher. I am Jesus Christ, the king you serve in your work. This day you have carried not only the whole world, but the one who created the world. In order that you might know what I say is true, place your staff in the earth by the house, and tomorrow it will bear flowers and fruit." Then the child disappeared.

The next morning Christopher walked outside, and there he found his staff bearing flowers, leaves, and dates. Christopher now knew that he served the greatest and most powerful master in the world.

Among the principles of spirituality embedded in this fable is the one of finding God where you are. Here is a man who could not fast and could not pray for long—these were not for him—but in his own gifts he found the Christ. He found his sanctity, as we would say, where he was planted. He uncovered his story where he was. In turn, he became a story for us to live by. So, we don't all have to follow only this or that way—say the rosary, join the Cursillo, etc. These are wonderful and work for many, but not for all. Your spiritual path may be different. The late Blessed Pope John XXIII put it well: "From the saints I must take the substance, not the accidents, of their virtues. I am not St. Aloysius, nor must I seek holiness in this particular way, but according to the requirements of my own nature, my own character, and the different conditions of my life" (*Journal of a Soul*).

45

The Legends of the Prophet Elijah

The prophet Elijah in Jewish lore is not only the prophet of biblical legend but also a bit of a trickster and magician. Well, one day, our story goes, he is walking through a town when he hears the sounds of a party coming from a very large and beautiful mansion. So he swirls around a couple of times and instantly he is clothed in the rags of a poor beggar. He goes and knocks on the door. After a while, the host, the head of the house, a grand man in his tuxedo answers. But he takes one look at Elijah's miserable clothing and immediately slams the door in his face, leaving Elijah sputtering.

Elijah goes away, swirls around a second time, and lo, is instantly clothed in the fine garments of a gentleman: white suit, ruffled shirt, top hat, spats, and a gold-handled cane. He knocks on the door. The host—the same man as before—answers. He takes one look at Elijah's splendid attire and ushers him in with a thousand welcomes.

Now at the feast there is a long table of the most exotic foods imaginable and the best wine from all over the world. Elijah goes immediately to the table and, in front of everybody, begins stuffing food into his shirt, into his jacket, into his pants pockets. The guests step back to watch this strange sight. Then he pushes more food into his shirt and finally takes the wine bottle and pours wine over his shoulders and down the front of his fine attire.

The host is shocked and irritated and shouts at Elijah, "What do you think you're doing?" Elijah replies, "I came to your door dressed in rags and you did not invite me in. Then I came to your door—the very same person—dressed in fine garments. Well, you welcomed me profusely to your feast. I could only conclude that it was not me that you invited but my clothes. So I fed them with your food and drink." Upon hearing this the people were ashamed and hung their heads. But when they looked up again, Elijah was gone and only his gold cane was left on the chair.

This is one of those "Ta-dah!" moments of insight that point out the right spiritual path.

Another legend about Elijah concerns a poor, blind, old man. He and his wife had no children. He had a hard life but never complained. One day Elijah came to him and told him, "Even though your life has been hard, you never complained, and so God will grant you one wish." The poor man smiled, "What a wish! What a wish! I am blind. I am poor, and I am childless. How can one wish satisfy all my problems? But," he sighed, "give me twenty-four hours and I'll come back with a wish."

So he went home and told his wife what had happened. She smiled at him and said, "Eat well and sleep soundly, for I know what you shall wish." So the man went back the next day and this is what he said to Elijah, "I wish to be able to see my children eat off gold plates."

The old trickster himself smiled. The wish was granted and the man and his wife lived happy for the rest of their days.

46

The Legend of St. Jerome

Here is a little legend about St Jerome, that crotchety scholar of the fifth century who fought with everyone (including the pope), translated the Bible into Latin, and lived in a cloister at Bethlehem with other monks.

One day a wounded lion appeared causing havoc and panic among all—except Jerome. The lion had a thorn in its paw and was in pain. Jerome took it out. The lion was grateful and became tame.

The problem was, what does one do with a tame lion? Some monks suggested that the lion keep watch over the donkey when he went into the woods to gather wood, although others said a lot of good that would do, for the lion, sooner or later, would pounce on the helpless donkey and eat him up. But this is what was decided and it worked out well. The lion kept the donkey safe from wild animals and protected him.

One day the lion fell asleep and some robbers came along, spied the donkey, and stole him. When the lion woke up and realized what had happened, he blamed himself and trotted back home. Some of the monks said, "Aha, we knew it! He ate the donkey." But Jerome said, "No, we don't know for sure. Let's not be hasty to judge." And the monks settled down under a cloud of suspicion.

One day, it so happened, while the lion was resting outside near a road, he saw a caravan—and who was leading it but the donkey! He was overjoyed. He ran to meet his old friend, scaring the hell out of the robbers. They fled to the nearest protection, the monks' cloister. There they fell down at the feet of Jerome and begged his forgiveness if only they would be spared. Moreover, they promised that whenever they came back that way they would provide for the monks.

The lion came, lay down, stretched out, and wagged its tail as if asking for forgiveness for a crime he never committed.

To this day, St. Jerome is pictured with a lion crouched at his feet.

47

The Legend of St. Genesius

Long ago in ancient Rome, Emperor Diocletian lounged on an ornately carved chair. Servants brought trays of food to tempt him, dancers twirled to delight him, and musicians played lively tunes to soothe his mood. The emperor yawned in boredom until the actors arrived. Then the emperor sat upright and cried out with delight, "Is Genesius here?"

"Indeed I am!" said a spry young man bounding forward. Genesius was a talented mime and a favorite performer of the emperor's. "Today," announced Genesius, "we will perform the comical play about the Christians." "Begin!" the emperor said, giggling in anticipation, for this was his favorite play. Since Genesius was especially good at doing impersonations, he easily parodied the characters of his day. The early Christians, whose rituals were unfamiliar to the emperor, were a prime target for Genesius' satire.

The emperor howled with delight as Genesius performed a mockery of the Christian rite of baptism. Another actor ceremoniously dunked Genesius in a huge tub of water, seeming to almost drown him. Genesius came sputtering and splashing wide-eyed out of the water. The emperor shouted, "Do it again!" Genesius suddenly stood silent and still. In the midst of the zany mockery, Genesius had in fact been converted to Christianity by the sacredness of the rite he ridiculed. "I cannot do the play again," Genesius said.

"But it is the funniest one! I command you to do it again!" the emperor insisted.

"No, I will not perform the play!" said Genesius, defying the emperor. "It would not be true to myself to mock what I now know is sacred."

This was courageous because Genesus knew what would happen. The emperor's face turned crimson with fury. "How dare you disobey me! Guards!" he bellowed. "Take this insolent man away and break his legs!" The guards dragged Genesius away and broke his legs.

In the Christian tradition, Genesius, the mime, became St. Genesius, the patron saint of performing artists. In modern times people sometimes offer encouragement to an actor who is about to go on stage by saying, "Break a leg!" Perhaps the expression refers to the story of St. Genesius and means "only perform that which is true to yourself," no matter what.

Good advice for would-be saints.

48

A Fable about Thou and I

Once long ago in a distant land, a prince was riding through a deep forest far from his home with his company of soldiers, looking for new lands to conquer. Quite suddenly he came upon a clearing in the trees. There before him stretched a meadow leading to a glorious hill. The meadow and hill were covered with blossoming trees, bushes, and wildflowers that seemed made of pure gold. It sparkled in the sunlight so brightly that the prince was nearly blinded.

Fascinated, the prince signaled to his regiment, and together they rode closer and closer, and up the hill toward a castle. The birds sang sweetly, the perfume of flowers was lovely. As they drew near the castle, he saw that a window opened for a moment in the wall and a face appeared, a face that shone more brilliantly than the sun and yet more gently than any flower. Then it was gone. Instantly he fell in love.

He knocked upon the castle door. "Who is there?" came a voice softer than the bluest sky. "It is I, Prince Rindleheart. I am known throughout the land for my bravery. My armies are the strongest, my wealth is enormous, my castle is but two days' ride from here. May I please come and be with you?" "There is only room for one of us here" was the reply.

He left downcast and in his desperation he sought the wisdom of a wise woman. "Perhaps your armies intimidate her," she suggested. "Of course," he thought. He returned to the castle alone and knocked upon the door. "Who is there?" came the sweet voice. "It is I, the mighty prince, alone," he replied. "There is only room for one of us here," said the sweet voice.

He went away again, dejected and confused. He roamed the wilderness for some years until he met a famous wizard. "Perhaps she cannot know you with all of your armor and weaponry," he suggested. "Of course!" said the prince. So he returned and laid down his armor, his shield, and his sword. He walked humbly to the castle door and knocked. "Who is there?" asked the voice. "It is I. No soldier, just a man." "There is only room for one of us here," came the reply.

For seven more years the prince wandered alone in the wilderness, forsaking his kingdom, thinking only of his beloved. He sought wisdom only from the stars in the sky and the wildness inside him.

Finally one day the prince returned to the castle on the hill. He had no armies, no armor, no horse, no nothing. He slowly walked up the hill, past the bushes heavily laden with fruit and knocked upon the door. "Who is there?" came the sweet voice. The prince took a breath—and said, "It is *thou.*"

And the door was opened to him.

Saints move from "it is I" to "it is Thou."

49

A Fable about Papa God

This is a delightful folktale from Haiti.

Once upon a time, in the middle of a great forest, there lived an old woman who kept hives of bees. By the end of the summer she had more honey than she could use: every jar, bowl, and barrel was filled to overflowing with the sweet golden honey. The old woman kept some for herself. The rest she poured into a great pot, lifted the pot on top of her head, and set off to market. Off she went through the great forest for days with the pot balanced on her head.

But just as she neared the marketplace she accidentally caught her foot on a tree root and went flying. There was a great crash. The pot had fallen and smashed to the ground oozing the sweet, sticky honey all over the forest floor. The woman just sat there and began to cry. "Oh misery!" she moaned, "Papa God, you sent me too much misery!" After a long while, she finally got up, trudged home with a heavy heart crying all the while, "Misery! Oh misery! Papa God, you sent me too much misery!"

Now it so happened that a little monkey, sitting high among the branches, saw the whole thing. As soon as the woman was out of sight, he swung down to the ground. He looked and looked at the strange sticky stuff. He had never seen anything like it before. Cautiously he dipped one of his fingers into it and touched his lips. "Oh, my," he exclaimed to himself, "this misery is good! I've never tried misery before." He scooped up a whole handful and swallowed it. He ate and ate until he got down to licking the pot until there simply wasn't any more. Oh, but there had to be more. "I want more!" he cried. And then he remembered overhearing the old woman saying. "Papa God, why'd you send me so much misery?" He scratched his head. So that's where misery came from! "Maybe," he thought to himself, "maybe if I paid Papa God a visit he'd give me some more misery." And the more he thought about it the better the idea seemed.

So off he went. Back to the trees and then to the mountains and he climbed and climbed until at last he came to Papa God's house. And there was Papa God himself sitting in the garden just watching the world. "Beg your pardon, Papa God," he shouted. Papa God turned and saw him and smiled. "Ah, little monkey, what do you want?"

"Begging your pardon, Papa God," said the little monkey, "more than anything else, I want misery." Papa God looked puzzled. "You want misery, little one?"

"Oh yes, sweet, sticky misery. I want as much as you can give me, Papa God."

Papa God got up, thought a minute, and said. "Well, it just so happens that I have got some special misery made just for monkeys. Are you sure you want it?" The monkey nodded his head. So Papa God went inside his house and, after a spell, returned carrying a leather bag. He said to the monkey, "Little monkey, this bag is full of misery. Now you must pay attention and do exactly what I tell you. First of all, you must carry this bag to the middle of a great sandy desert where there are no trees and where, in fact, they can't grow. Then, once you're there, you will slowly open the bag and inside you'll find more misery than you ever dreamed of."

The monkey was delighted and wasted no time. He took the leather bag and climbed back down to the world, and he ran and ran until he came to the edge of a great desert, and then he ran and ran some more until he came to its very center. Exhausted, he sat down. His hands were trembling in anticipation of all that misery. So he opened the drawstrings of the bag just as Papa God had told him and out came real monkey misery…DOGS! One, two, three, up to seven huge, hungry black dogs! The monkey screamed, dropped the bag and ran literally for his life. The seven black dogs were snapping at his tail. They were getting closer and closer. And just when he thought he could go no further and the dogs were sure to get him…. a tree appeared!

Out of nowhere a huge, great tree appeared, right there in the middle of the desert where trees, of course, do not grow at all. The monkey scampered up the tree as fast as he could leaving the seven snarling dogs leaping up and down the trunk.

And for the rest of the day he sat in the tree branches quaking with fear until the sun went down and the dogs, frustrated, eventually slunk away. As soon as they were gone and the monkey thought it was safe, he climbed down and ran for the forest as fast as he could and never looked back.

Now the question—the sainthood question—is this: where did that tree come from? Who put that great tree where trees don't grow, right there in the middle of a hot, dry desert? I'll tell you. Papa God put it there. Why? Because Papa God knows that too much misery is not a good thing, even for a monkey.

And that is the meaning of the fable. We are in a desert full of miseries. So much war and poverty and corruption in high places. Greed and betrayals abound in government, the professions, in our own church. Too much misery is not good for us monkeys, so Papa God in his mercy in each and every age raises up saints where you least expect them and where you would not expect them to grow. But there they are.

These are the saints we have met and there are so many more still among us. They are unexpected graces. The saints give us hope, for in them we do catch a glimpse of what God is like and what we are called to be.

50

A Fable about the Hedly Kow

It happened that an old woman, Mrs. Miller, was on her way back home from market one day, trudging peacefully through the twilight, thinking of her nice, warm fireside, when she saw something lying in the road ahead. "Why, it's a pot, a big iron pot. It must have fallen off someone's wagon. Or else there's a hole in it somewhere, and so it's been just thrown away. A good, useful thing like that—why, I can use it, hole or no hole, to plant some flowers in."

But when she looked in the pot, the old woman gasped. "Gold pieces! The pot is full of gold pieces! Why, what a lucky woman I am!" Tying her sturdy woolen shawl around the pot, she began to drag the heavy thing home. But something felt very strange about her burden. And when she turned around to see what was wrong, the old woman gasped again.

"My eyes must have played a trick on me. How could I ever have mistaken that for a mass of gold coins? It's a lump of silver. Better and better! If I tried to spend all of those coins, folks would wonder where I got them. They might even think I was a thief! No, no, a lump of silver will be much simpler to sell. Why, what a lucky woman I am!"

Off she went again, dragging the lump of silver behind her. But once more, something felt very strange about it, and she turned around to see what was wrong. "Now, isn't this the silliest thing? My eyes really are playing tricks on me. How could I have thought this was a lump of silver when it's a nice mass of iron, good, solid iron. Better and better yet! Silver would be odd to sell, and folks would still be wondering if I was a thief, but iron, well, any ironsmith will gladly buy it from me. What a lucky woman I am!"

Off she went again, dragging the mass of iron after her. But once more, something felt very strange about her burden, and she turned to see what was wrong. "Oh, my. Oh, dear. Oh, my dear. It must be the dim twilight fooling me, that's what it is. That's no mass of iron I'm pulling along, it's a good, heavy stone. A nice, smooth, round one, too—exactly what I've been needing to prop open my door. What a lucky woman I am!"

She hurried home with her prize and set it beside the door. But no sooner had she untied the shawl from the rock than "Whoosh!" The rock was suddenly growing, sprouting ears and legs and a long donkey tail. Before the old woman could so much as gasp, the creature was gone into the night, braying and laughing. "Oh, my dear, dear me, that was no stone, that was the Hedley Kow! And to think I had a chance to see him. What a lucky, lucky woman I am!"

An old English folktale that pleasantly sounds the theme of holy detachment.

51

Mr. Holland and the Holy Shadow
• A FINAL HOMILY •

When the feast of St. Albert the Great fell, I couldn't help but remark to the people that there was not a big hurrah over the fact. Who in the world knows Albert the Great? Who ever heard of him? Yes, he was a good and holy man but I suspect he got into the calendar more because of his pupil, that fat kid who seemed dull enough to earn the snotty title of "the dumb ox" among his peers. His pupil was St. Thomas Aquinas, who was to become one the most brilliant and famous theologians in the Catholic Church. Albert didn't know that at the time.

Life is like that, full of second fiddles. People who pass on love, truth, and tradition and never see what comes of it. Teachers and parents fit here. They often don't see the fruit of their efforts. Once in a while, years and years later, you might meet a pupil who poses to you the astounding question: did you ever realize how much of an impact you had on them? How often they recalled the things you taught them? No you didn't. It happens, but not often. Most of us are not Thomas Aquinases. Most of us are Alberts, doing our best and seldom getting to see the results.

But I tell you, it's a noble and holy state of affairs: trusting that what you scattered will catch hold and, day by day, shape disciples, without always knowing if any of them followed you. For most of us our task is to pass on faith, hope, and love, fully realizing that we will not always know how they caught on, if we have influenced anyone for the better. We scatter seeds. We're not always there to see the outcome. We don't need to. We've done God's task and that's all that matters.

All this calls to mind that the other night, while surfing the television, I caught my favorite channel, Turner Classic Movies. It was showing *Mr. Holland's Opus*, a terrific movie featuring Richard Dreyfuss, who deservedly was nominated for an Oscar for it. You recall the movie. Let me describe is as best as I can remember for those who don't.

Mr. Holland is a music teacher who desperately needs to make ends meet, especially since his only son was born deaf and needs special care. So he signs on to teach at a local high school. This puts his great ambition on hold a while: to work on his dream concerto. Now he can only do it in dribs and drabs because kids who need help keep popping up. And so for thirty years the concerto is on the back burner while the needs and demands of the students absorb his time.

After thirty years the school, in a budget crunch, is forced to cut back, and the first to go is the music program. On the last day Mr. Holland is clearing out his room with his wife and son and, as they are leaving, they hear some noise coming from the large auditorium. Curious, they go over, and as they enter they see the place filled to capacity—and it's filled with Mr. Holland's students from the past thirty years, many coming great distances. There is a huge, thunderous applause, and the stunned Mr. Holland is led to the front. Finally the door opens again and in comes the governor of the state, one of Mr. Holland's pupils, whom he helped out when she needed encouragement. She goes up to the stage to the microphone and when all are seated she begins by saying something like, "Mr. Holland, we all know that for thirty years you worked on your concerto but never got to finish it because so many students needed you. I understand that you consider yourself something of a failure. But I tell you, Mr. Holland, you are not. There is no one in this auditorium who has not been affected by you, whom you have not touched, for whom you have not made a difference. Mr. Holland, you are a success. We are your notes. We are your music." And then the stage curtain opens and there is a full orchestra and the governor invites Mr. Holland to come up and conduct his concerto.

On the spiritual journey that's the path most of us tread, we reach out to touch and mold the hearts and lives of others, and we do not always see the outcome. But we don't always need to, It's our calling and it is precious. An old Sufi story called "The Holy Shadow" spells it out.

As everybody knows, goes the tale, the Angelic Council meets on Wednesday afternoons from 3:00 to 5:00 to consider earthly candidates for special gifts, rewards, and honors. The list of potential recipients is usually long and a lot of "weeding out" is necessary.

Well, after one particularly tedious meeting, the potential recipient for the week was selected and the name was sent "upstairs." The Angelic Council, of course, is purely advisory to the Divine Source, who has to give the final OK to each nominee. This time a memo came down that said, "Approved, but ask her first."

The Angelic Council selected a subcommittee. They immediately flew to earth and found their potential recipient. In a formal and solemn presentation, they offered her a gift. "You have been found worthy," they said in unison. (With so much time spent in the angelic choir, angels always speak in unison.) "We are pleased to give you the gift of healing touch. Whomever you lay your hands upon will be healed." The woman said that she was sure the gift of healing touch was very much needed in the world in which she lived, but she declined the honor. "Perhaps someone else would accept it," she said. The angels quickly caucused. Being superior beings, they adjusted their plans to meet the situation and returned with a new offer.

"You have been found worthy," they said in unison. "We are pleased to give you the gift of conversion of hearts. Whenever you speak, people will be moved to change their lives for the better." "I am sure that the gift of conversion of hearts is very much needed in the world in which I live," replied the woman, "but someone else must accept that gift. I decline the honor."

Grumbling now, the angels caucused a second time. They returned with a new proposal. "You have been found worthy," they said in unison. "We are pleased to give you the gift of great virtue. People will see your deeds and be encouraged to live lives of high moral values." The woman agreed that the gift of great virtue was very much needed in the world in which she lived, but she insisted that someone else needed to receive it. She declined once again.

It was only after the woman's third refusal that the angels remembered what the divine memo has said: "Ask her first." "So, if you don't want the healing touch, the gift of the conversion of hearts, or great virtue, what is it you do want?" the angels asked in frustrated unison. The woman answered quickly, for she always knew what she wanted. "I want the gift of doing good," she said, "but not knowing it. "

The angels caucused. This was a new and unforeseen request. They were energized and buzzing with the challenge, their wings beating excitedly. After some time, they came upon the way that the "gift of doing good but not knowing it" could be bestowed. They made the woman's shadow a source of goodness. She would go about her life doing what had to be done, but whatever or whomever her shadow fell upon would be graced. As she walked by a withered brook and her shadow fell across it, for example, it would suddenly gurgle with sweet, clear, running water. If her shadow fell upon a sullen child, the child would suddenly smile contentedly. If she passed a world-weary man, he would reawaken to vital purpose and passion.

And so the woman would live, going about doing good and not knowing it. The people in her world respected the humility of the woman. They never told her of the healing effects of her shadow, although many tried to walk behind her. And since her good deeds were never explicitly attributed to her, her name has been forgotten. She is remembered only as the "Holy Shadow."

This old Sufi story is a reminder to see oneself as a "holy shadow," a medium of grace and not as its source. We must do our best and leave the rest in the hands of God.

This, by the way, is a good story for parents. For some parents, their hearts are broken when they see their children turning out poorly: drugs, divorce, criminal activity, and so on. "Where did I go wrong?" they ask themselves. They feel guilty. For them is it healing to consider the Good Thief on the cross next to Jesus. That young man led a despicable life and disappointed his parents, who must have lived in shame to see how their son turned out. But they never ceased praying for him. It turns out that they were never to know in this life that their unceasing prayers and early teaching sparked a last minute confession and an unexpected openness to grace. The moral? Keep on scattering the seeds of prayer for your wayward children.

A PRAYER TO END WITH

God has created me to do him some definite service.
He has committed some work to me that he has not
*   committed to another.*
I have my mission.
I may never know it in this life
but I shall be told it in the next.
I am a link in a chain,
a bond of connection between persons.
He has not created me for naught;
I shall do good—I shall do his work;
I shall be an angel of peace,
a preacher of truth in my own place while not
*   intending it*
if I do but keep his commandments.
Therefore I will trust him.
Whatever I am, I can never be thrown away.
If I am in sickness, my sickness may serve him;
in perplexity, my perplexity may serve him.
If I am in sorrow, my sorrow may serve him.
He does nothing in vain. He knows what he is about.
He may take away my friends,
He may throw me among strangers,
He may make me feel desolate,
make my spirits sink, hide my future from me—still
He knows what he is about.

BLESSED CARDINAL NEWMAN

NOTES AND CREDITS

The sources of this anthology are listed here. But not all. The trouble is that I, like so many others, have heard or read the stories of the saints over the years, stories frequently unmoored by memory, time, and custom from their original sources and authorship. Their origins remain difficult to track down. I have made every effort to give credit and will welcome any further information.

Introduction
The quotation from Lawrence Cunningham is from his book, *Things Seen and Unseen* (Sorin Books, Notre Dame, 2010, p. 38.)

2. The Saintly Underground
This chapter is not intended to undermine the institutional Church. It's role in worldwide charity, care, and education is second to none. It's just that the Church as institution, the Church as identified with the hierarchy, gets bad press and some of it is justified. The chapter is really a variation on the old canard that "if it doesn't happen in the parish, it doesn't happen."

3. The Saintly Contagion
The Ellsberg quote is from *The Saints' Guide to Happiness* (Image Books, 2005).

10. St. Catherine of Genoa and St. Joan of Oregon
Joan Ryan's account is to be found in Voice of the Faithful newsletter, October, 2005.

11. St. Callixtus of Rome
The sources for St. Callixtus are mostly from Thomas Craughwell's book, *Saints Behaving Badly*, plus Internet sources.

13. St. Catherine of Siena
The best source is *Catherine of Siena: A Passionate Life* by Don Brophy (Bluebridge Press, 2011).

16. Harriet Tubman

Material comes from *8 Freedom Heroes* by Brennan R. Hill (St. Anthony Messenger Press, 2007) and other sources.

17. Thomas Merton

The material is largely inspired by James Martin's book, *My Life with the Saints* (Loyola Press, 2007).

18. Dorothy Day

Material comes from Robert Ellsberg including his article in *America* (November 15, 2010) and James Martin's book, *My Life with the Saints*. The movie alluded to starred Martin Sheen and Moira Kelly. For an excellent dramatic summary of Dorothy Day's life check out Sarah Melici's one-woman show on DVD called *Fool for Christ* (foolforchrist.com)

22. Saintly Snapshots

The Dr. DeBakey bio comes from an article in *TIME* magazine (July 19, 2004) and Dr. Lena Edwards from Camille Lewis Brown, *African Saints, African Stories* (St. Anthony Messenger Press, 2008). The Sito story is from *The Four Gospel Journey as a Guide for the Spiritual Life* by Alexander J. Shaia, published by Now You Know Media (Copyright ©2010 by Now You Know Media. Used herewith by permission of Now You Know Media, Inc.).

24. Mother Mary MacKillop

Sources are *Our Sunday Visitor*, October, 17, 2010, "Saints: Rebel with a Cause" by Thomas J. Craughwell, *The Tablet* (October 23, 2010) and my friend, Australian priest Father Pat Connor, SVD.

26. Miguel Pro

Sources are Creighton University, Catholic News Agency, EWTNews, American Catholic.org, and other internet sources.

29. Florence and Edith

Sources for Edith Cavell are *The Tablet* (November 13, 2010), Legends and Traditions of the Great War, Wikipedia, and other Internet sources.

30. Augustus Tolton

Sources: *National Catholic Reporter* (November 26, 2010, p. 20) and Internet sources such as rootsweb.ancestry.com, holyangels.com, and Wikipedia.

31. Victoria Rasomanarivo

Sources are *African Saints, African Stories* by Camille Lewis Brown (St. Anthony Messenger Press, 2008) and Internet sources.

33. Mother Teresa

I am indebted for my remarks to James Martin, SJ, a Jesuit priest and author of *My Life with the Saints*. I have written what is basically a homiletic version of his article "In My Soul" (*America,* September 24, 2007, p. 14ff).

34. St. Damien of Molokai

Sources are *Leper Priest of Moloka'i* by Hilde Eynikel (Alba House, Staten Island, 1999) and *The Spirit of Father Damien* by Jan De Volder (Ignatius Press, 2010).

36. Paul Rusesabagina and the Benebikira Sisters

Sources: *National Catholic Reporter* (October 28, 2010), nationalgeographic.com/news, Wikipedia, and other Internet sources.

38. Oscar Romero

Sources: "The Ongoing Legacy of Archbishop Oscar Romero," *St. Anthony Messenger* (December, 2010), Wikipedia, and other Internet sources.

40. St. Dad

Source: From *Wisdom of Our Fathers* by Tim Russert, copyright ©2007 by Tim Russert. Used by permission of Random House, Inc.

41. The Legend of St. Alexander

From *Sixty Saints for Boys* by Joan Windham, copyright 1999. Reproduced by kind permission of Continuum International Publishing Group.

51. Mr Holland and The Holy Shadow

The Holy Shadow story comes from the creative pen of Fr. Ed Hayes.